INTERIOR DESIGN AND BEYOND

INTERIOR DESIGN AND BEYOND

ART • SCIENCE • INDUSTRY

MARY V. KNACKSTEDT, ASID, IFDA

With Laura J. Haney

JOHN WILEY & SONS, INC.

New York ■ Chichester ■ Brisbane ■ Toronto ■ Singapore

We would like to hear your comments. For further information on seminars and other products, call, write, or fax Mary Knackstedt at 2901 N. Front St., Harrisburg, PA 17110 (717) 238-7548 FAX (717) 233-7374

This text is printed on acid-free paper.

This publication is designed to provide accurate and authoritative information in regard to the subject matter covered. It is sold with the understanding that the publisher is not engaged in rendering legal, accounting, or other professional services. If legal advice or other expert assistance is required, the services of a competent professional person should be sought.

Library of Congress Cataloging-in-Publication Data:
Knackstedt, Mary V.
    Interior design & beyond : art, science, industry   /   Mary
V. Knackstedt with Laura J. Haney.
        p.   cm.
    Includes bibliographical references and index.
    ISBN 0-471-11834-6
    1. Interior decoration—United States—History—20th century.
2. Interior decorators—United States—Psychology.   3. Interior
decoration firms—United States—Management.   I. Haney, Laura J.
II. Title.   III. Title: Interior design and beyond.
NK2004.K58   1995
729'.068—dc20   94-45550

Printed in the United States of America

10 9 8 7 6 5 4 3 2 1

CONTENTS

INTRODUCTION

Interior design affects everyone. It has the power to direct movement and interaction, enhance vision and hearing, and inspire emotion. And it is taken for granted, even by people who practice it. Interior design has been and will always be practiced in partnership with other disciplines, but in creating interiors, interior designers orchestrate what these disciplines do.

Interior design can make it possible for people to do better at whatever they attempt, with the right environments. This is power, and with it comes great responsibility, because interior design can direct behavior. Bad design, or lack of design, can contribute to social unrest. Good design makes people's movements more effective and their lives more comfortable and pleasurable. Other professions, mostly in the sciences, have documented the effects of things interior designers learned by doing and by instinct.

Most interior designers regard this power, and the responsibility that comes with it, too casually. I am not sure the term "interior design" is strong enough to convey the responsibility of our profession.

It is time to acknowledge that interior design has evolved into a profession that can affect the way we live like no other profession. We have the training to accept the responsibility. Our work has the potential to affect the way people live for generations. We have the opportunity to create living spaces that are healthier, better support a range of human activities, and inspire behavior that is more socially acceptable. What a challenge, and what an exciting profession we work in!

I speak from experience. I was born into this industry and have spent over 35 years working in the design field, both as a designer and as a business consultant to other designers. This broad exposure to the effects of design work has taught me to respect the potential for the field.

I am also an optimist and an instigator. Seeing the potential for interior design, I want us all to benefit from it. Interior design today is a whole new game, and it's thrilling.

MARY KNACKSTEDT

This book combines the work and beliefs of two people who have worked in the design industry for years, yet it is written with one voice.

We started this book from different directions. Mary wanted to rouse the interior design field from its passive/reactor position, and I wanted to remind designers about the social and behavioral aspects of the work. Through heated discussion we found that we could do both.

Why has the interior design profession taken the role of a reactor to events rather than that of an actor? We think it is because interior designers lost the strength of their conviction that interior design can make the world better. The economy of the past few years thinned out the number of design practitioners. Interior designers started to believe other professions when they belittled the effects of interior design. Despite the eminently practical nature of interior design, the aesthetic component is what gets media notice, and perhaps the field began to believe its own press.

Interior Design & Beyond puts the role of interior design in a new perspective, that of instigator. We believe that interior design can change the world, not just make life prettier for a select few. We also believe that reading this book will give you the background to start changing the way you practice, thereby changing the way the public thinks about interior design.

Interior design is essential. It affects the quality of life. Good design can reduce stress. You shouldn't have the constant stress of fighting your environment. As Mary says, knowing how to improve the way people live makes it our responsibility to do so.

LAURA J. HANEY

1

A STARTING POINT

Reasonable men adapt themselves to their environment; unreasonable men try to adapt their environment to themselves. Thus all progress is the result of the efforts of the unreasonable men.
GEORGE BERNARD SHAW

THE UNREASON IN OUR SOULS

The interior design discipline can grow exponentially, or it can self-destruct. There are many areas of our field that require alterations and adjustments. Our industry needs to plan for change to meet needs and to approach the opportunities of tomorrow.

We are designers. We're in this field because we have vision and the ability to design and create a room or a building. Now we must do the same thing with our field. It is time for major changes. We've known it for a long time. This field does not work well today. It does not suit our current market. We need to start thinking about transforming our field. This book provides a new system of thinking.

AN INDUSTRY IN TURMOIL

Right now our industry, furnishings and design, is in chaos. The market we had is gone and a new market is forming. Interior design firms and the interior design industry may survive but not as they are currently structured.

I look at our field and see that things aren't working right. I see organizations in change and wonder whether those changes are right for the field and right for our clients. I wonder about our need and purpose, and I think about surviving and dealing with the changes and issues that are part of our client's lives. We have to keep a positive attitude if we're going to help our clients.

It's not just a question of competition, quality of work, or ability. New technology and changes in the demand for interior design mean interior design firms and the entire furnishings and design industry must function differently.

So much of what is wrong in our industry comes not from outside forces but from our own thinking and the way we and our firms operate. Our situation reminds me of the frog and the pot. If you put a frog in a pot and turn up the heat slightly every few minutes, the frog will eventually be boiled to death without really being aware of what was going on.

This is what I've seen happening to our field. We don't recognize the problems because they occurred as a long, slow process, but problems exist and the field needs a dramatic change to survive. As an industry, we have been reactors, not initiators. Reacting is not the only purpose of design. Design is creating change.

Our industry is not the only one in transition. Theories on business management pop up faster than you can say "Total Quality Management," "Reengineering the Corporation" or "Rethinking the Corporation." Thank goodness they've taken the place of concepts of winning through intimidation and manipulation. So many businesses focus on the next quarter's profits, not on why they are in business in the first place.

Winston Churchill said, "We make a living by what we get. We make a life by what we give." We'll be looking more at what we give in this next decade—what we give to our clients and the people we work with, what we give to our community, and what we give to our world.

And I think this will give us back the reasons we are in this industry. We have worked hard to be efficient and profitable. Some of these attempts have sapped our dedication to our work, and we have lost something vital.

This turmoil, this struggle to survive is an opportunity for individuals to find purpose and meaning in their work. For our profession to be as rewarding as it ought to be, we need to restructure our value systems and priorities. We have to do this with vision and with an accurate picture of the current reality.

There are trends our industry can't ignore, both nationwide and global. Downsizing and technology have cut the workforce and changed the way people work. There is a new decentralization of power and an increase in cooperative effort. An estimated 41 million Americans now do some work at home. Consumer awareness and concern for energy-efficient products, protecting the environment, and indoor air quality have pushed manufacturers in a new direction. There is a national accessibility law, the Americans with Disabilities Act. There's the whole electro-techno revolution, with portable communications systems and information via computers, fax and cellular phones. And there is the competition from 800 telephone numbers and shopping on television. This is just the beginning.

Douglas MacArthur said, "There is no security on this earth. There is only opportunity."

We have an opportunity to change our field, to put back into it the heart and soul and passion, to fulfill our desire to make people's lives better through design. It will take a great deal of dedication, a strong core belief, a willingness to play the game, and a willingness to take on the responsibility.

The routine business structures that have occupied so much of our time have destroyed part of our creativity. We can't continue to blindly fix the structures as new theories pop up. We have to determine whether our business structure is worth saving in the first place.

After I read *Reengineering the Corporation* (Hammer and Champy, 1993) I thought about how it applied to our field. There is no question that our field is worth saving. Interior design is an art and a science, and it has developed into something far more complex than choosing fabric and colors. We need to recognize that design encompasses a broad range of activities and entails a great many responsibilities. Interior design is more valuable now than it has ever been.

I'm not going to throw away everything I've worked to learn since design school. I'm going to redesign my business so that it contains some fun, so that the work itself is part of the reward. And I think we all have to do this. Our field needs to meet the needs of today so it does not become a dinosaur.

I have worked in this field a long time. I'm constantly asking questions and looking at new directions. I know I don't have all the answers, but I hope this book will encourage interior designers to start dealing with our opportunities and to really see that we, as designers, can be agents for change in this world of ours.

THE FUTURE IS THE PAST

The future is really the good old standards of the past. Teamwork and acting from a sense of responsibility are the new paradigm, the new model for a working ethic. This change is an opportunity for individuals to find purpose and meaning in their work.

One observer called the change in the business ethic the spiritual awakening of the Baby Boomers, but it is more a reassertion of the values that existed before all the manipulative formulas for success came into fashion. No matter what name you call it, there is a new and stronger emphasis on relationships and responsibility.

This permits us to deal with the real values. In the near future, Americans will be very sensitive to the ecology and what we cost the ecology. We will act as stewards rather than as consumers. Long-term efficiency will be valued over short-term answers, both in business and in our personal lives. In other words, we should examine our actions in terms of what will be healthful and helpful to people who work with us, our clients and the world.

We'll be looking to nature as a partner. We won't have to fight the sun and the moisture level, because our designs will work *with* them.

This new pattern for business offers different career choices. Technology and knowledge make individual workers more responsible for the outcome of their work. This results in decentralization of power, and a cooperative effort that we have not seen recently. It *did* exist in mom-and-pop businesses. When you are responsible for the results of your work, you develop pride in your work and a concern for quality. This personal power goes beyond Total Quality Management.

The scale of business will return to a more human dimension. Companies will not be as large, and there will be fewer traditional large, global operations. Even global corporations will be made up of many small firms. Each division performs independently but is linked, as states are to the federal government.

Accounting systems are changing. It's not simply a matter of cash assets, return on investment, or short-term profits. To meet the challenges of our changing industry, we need knowledge and people with ability. Wealth and assets are redefined to take into consideration knowledge, social issues and social accounting.

PEOPLE POWER

Today, a company is not the sum total of its capital assets and equipment. It is intellectual capital that counts. Workers are a prime asset; having a well-trained staff is essential. Equipment becomes obsolete, sometimes within months or days or hours. People are able to adapt; people can gain new knowledge; people are resourceful and creative. And this flexibility can be directed into earnings, whereas a piece of equipment that is obsolete is just so much junk that you have to pay people to haul away.

People want to work in a world where they see value. Making money is less important than being part of creating something that has real value. Interior designers want to create environments that meet needs and give us something to be proud of.

Just as we try to preserve and protect the ecology, we also have to preserve and protect our human assets. In the 1980s the "flight" of young professionals into jobs that left time for family and friends was a common topic in newspapers. Americans now care about doing things other than work, and corporations are beginning to recognize this.

Time is a factor. We want to invest our time in something we see as worthwhile. A goal must be accomplished in a reasonable amount of time.

Futurists tell us that in the fourth wave, business will emerge as a leader of society and will be responsible for the whole world. In the past, other social institutions were responsible. Today businesses and business organizations stand the greatest chance of being able to make changes.

Owning things is not a reward in itself. We used to think it would be wonderful to own a car or a house, but ownership takes away some of our freedom, flexibility, and opportunity to do other things. Perhaps having seven cars and six houses takes more management than it is worth.

Ownership is an obligation, and in the future we will need to be more cautious as to how we dedicate our obligations. Do we dedicate ourselves to a thing or to an opportunity and a challenge? Do we want to spend our lives owning things or doing things?

We will be looking not just at what we want but at what our clients want. It is not what we think they want, but what they *really* want. Change is one thing that will be consistent, which is why with the benefit of technology and this type of structure we can manage changes easily.

We will be looking at target markets. We cannot service everyone in every area. We will see our companies becoming far more specialized and therefore focused on a particular type of client. We will therefore structure the firm both in knowledge base and technology to support that market.

We will elect to use fewer resources and have smaller staffs. Many staff members will have to change to keep up with the market. Technology gives us an opportunity to bring in high quality staff people who are not necessarily on our weekly payrolls, yet are still a part of our company.

The terms that keep popping up again and again are: relationships, focus, specialized, business-driven by what we do. Many of the old terms that were part of our practice will be replaced by these and other new terms.

The greatest privilege anyone can give me is the opportunity to work, to create within my discipline, and to use my enthusiasm and the skills of my profession. Considering the expanding opportunities, what a challenge!

2

A PASSION TO DESIGN

I don't know a real designer who works only for a paycheck. Every one of us wants to be doing something we believe in. There is the design excitement in being part of a special project. There is a visible result. We're happy to be going to work every morning. It's not a case of getting up and thinking, "I've got to be there by 8:30." We all anticipate going to work because once we get there we are working on something worthwhile. Each project can be worthy of our talent and effort.

Not everyone is totally self-motivated, *but* if they are part of an exciting project, they become motivated, they get caught up in the excitement of it. Most designers like to talk about their work. They are excited to tell you what they are doing. They are passionate. They're enthusiastic. They're committed to what they do. Interior design is definitely more than a job—it's really a mission, an excitement, or a religion. There is no greater natural high.

THE DESIGN SPIRIT

It's time to recognize the value of interior design. Interior designers know what design can do. We're excited by it. We are willing to exert every effort required to give our clients the special environments that will permit them to perform better with greater ease and enjoyment. This is the core, the soul, the mission of interior design. It is the understanding and belief in that mission that gives design new spirit.

I see this spirit, this energy, in chapter after chapter of design organizations, from design center to design center, throughout this country. I have now conducted workshops in all but four states, and I have seen many different styles of practicing interior design. Although the process and style of work often differ due to client, climate or geography, this spirit, attitude, and excitement form a common denominator. Interior designers share the belief that the world is going to be a better place because they have been here. You see this spirit in successful design centers and design firms. When the spirit is gone, the design industry seems dead.

I want to be part of a team that is winning. This enhances the joy of doing. Interior design as an industry and a profession is misunderstood. Because it is fun, many people see it as a hobby and it really isn't just that—it's serious art, science, and philosophy. Only when these are combined is the process really successful.

DESIGNER AS COACH-TRAINER

Today almost everyone believes that they are interior designers, and this is true . . . just as there are people who believe they know how to exercise and people who exercise with personal trainers. Professional trainers help people spend exercise time wisely, resulting in well-shaped bodies. In the same way, professional design trainers can help people shape their choices according to their abilities.

Most clients want control over their own lives and their environments. So the role of the interior designer has changed, and interior design must be performed in partnership with the client, a partnership similar to that of a coach or a personal trainer. A design trainer assists individuals, companies and associations by expanding their opportunities and exposing them to experiences, materials and techniques they have never seen. This improves performance levels.

One thing design can do is to improve health and comfort with furnishings that support physical needs. Design techniques can create specific psychological effects. Your work as a designer/trainer may include giving clients the opportunity to express the culture of their personal business or social attitude.

Both the design client and the interior design professional must accept the responsibility of their positions and play their roles accordingly. The process of design is a refined discipline, not a helter-skelter process. It is too easy to be led down a blind alley. Good communication between designer and client enhances the project. Focusing on the project and sharing information to achieve the common goal of a good project can be almost a spiritual experience and can result in projects that symbolize the best of the art and science of interior design.

As designers we have the opportunity and the skills to create spaces that perform and nurture. So much in life is beyond control. With interior design we can create controlled environments. We need to take this seriously, to create spaces for our clients that complement their personalities and enhance the activities they will perform in these spaces.

THE CHALLENGE

Fortunately, business operates more efficiently in a changing period than any other social institution. A business is focused and productive. Today our business faces a challenge that demands all of our inner spirit, our intuition, our sensitivity, the knowledge we have, and our faith.

We can no longer afford to look at people as if they were easily replaceable and in need of constant supervision. We have to look at people in terms of potential, as team players who may become masters, designers and leaders of teams. We must develop our team players into master performers.

We want to be part of making the world better. In the coming decade we will look more at what we give to our clients, our communities, and the world. Ownership alone is unfulfilling.

Today many well educated and brilliant people, people who are apparently successful, are looking for meaning in their lives. Joy in working is a major component of life. It's what made us designers. If we no longer enjoy designing, we have lost a great deal of our excitement in life.

We have to look at the true meaning of our profession, and we have the ability to improve the life styles of our clients and others we come into contact with. Recently the profession has been so focused on high volume and production that design was no longer fun.

When your main purpose in being in business is to make money, I don't think you can attain the performance levels possible when you are in business because you love it. In the past few decades we have been consumed with economic production and acquisition. Most businesses have been guided by what affects their corporations in the next quarter.

Can we return a profession that has become an industrial, very mechanical, detached way of working to a profession that works with emotion? Will that emotion give us back the spirit and soul and special excitement that leads to higher and higher performance levels?

WHAT ABOUT THE CASH?

There is a book titled *Do What You Love . . . The Money Will Follow.*

The truth is that enthusiasm and good feelings are attractive and contagious. If you love your work and show it, people are drawn to you and your business.

I have a few favorite restaurants I go to, week in and week out. Recently I went in on a Saturday night, the usual night for eating out and this place was almost empty. Another restaurant told me that no tables would be available. What's the story? The food is good, the service is good. The owner learned the restaurant business at his father's knee, and his father has been very successful at every restaurant he ever ran.

The son went to college and his father had little formal education. The son's decision to go into the restaurant business was based on a belief that with his brains and background he'd be a millionaire in no time. The son had several restaurants and none of them has been a goldmine. His father is in the business because he loves it. Two months ago he bought back a restaurant that wasn't doing well. It was producing $3500 a week in gross sales. In less than a month, it does that much in a day.

I bet you anything the son and his father have totally different personalities. The son went into the business for the bottom line, and his father is in it because he loves the challenge and the social contact.

The point is that if you worry too much about the financial aspects of the work, it gets in the way. You cannot be worrying about the money for the payroll on Thursday afternoon or Friday. You have to feel pretty comfortable with finances to be able to concentrate on design and run the rest of the business. When money becomes more important than anything else, it is a stress. You can lose your creativity, your excitement, and your ability to produce.

In every course I've led and in my other books, I have tried to make managing a company comfortable to a designer. Even though a lot what I wrote was about money, the message was to be comfortable with it.

KEEP YOUR EYES ON REALITY

You cannot profit from the opportunities of a changing market unless you recognize current needs. These are thrown in front of us daily by newspapers and television. Although the situation seems overwhelming, great things are possible if you work on a small area at a time. Keep your eye on the reality of today as well as that of the future. If you don't understand reality, you cannot make good or timely decisions.

Look at what is real, what affects you, and the parameters of your decisions. Business in general has not been dedicated to working with nature as a partner. We have not really been dedicated to our work. We have been encouraged to look at what our work can do for us, how little time we can spend doing it, and how little effort we can put into it. Unfortunately, we have been looking at the easy way of doing things and accepting cookie-cutter solutions rather than designing. The easy way is not exciting, fun, or innovative. We need to do better for our clients and for ourselves.

YOUR ENTHUSIASM INDEX

Remember how excited you were when you started out as a designer, the passion you had? Do you still have it?

It's a good idea to look at your career and review essential issues every six months:

- Are you passionate and excited about what you're doing? Do you get as much fun out of it as you used to? Does this still turn you on? Is this really what you want to be doing?
- Are you achieving your goals and objectives? Is this what you thought you wanted to do?
- If your objectives have changed, have they changed in the right direction?
- Is this a job for you, or is it a career? Does it meet your expectations?
- Are you really doing what you are good at, or are you spending too much time doing things that you don't enjoy and are not good at? If that time and energy had been spent on design, it could have enriched your design work and made you feel better about your career.
- What are the rewards? Is there the satisfaction, excitement, joy, and rewards you want from this career?
- Is this where you want to be? Is this where you belong?
- Are you growing as a designer?
- Remember that the smile in your voice and the bounce in your step are what clients find attractive.

Great designers are alight with creative energy. If you are not happy at what you are doing and the way it's going, do something about it. Maybe you ought to take a year (or some other block of time) away from your work. Borrow the money from a bank, if necessary. Then when you return to your design firm, you'll be the enthusiastic designer clients want to hire. No one really wants a designer who is just marking time. Clients want designers who bring some excitement and joy as well as creativity to their project.

3

REALITY CHECK
Business Theories and Their Effect on the Workplace

It is the nature of man as he grows older to protest against change, particularly change for the better.
JOHN STEINBECK

In the introduction I wrote that the design industry is in chaos. Our industry is in chaos partly because technology permitted business management systems worldwide to move away from the method used for two hundred years and toward a new one. It's not just our industry, it is every industry. The old theory, division of labor, changed through the use of technology, and the focus was lost.

If business is to be effective, we have to reexamine all of the processes created by the division of labor and eliminate any that no longer work. Technology and changes in demand require a new company structure, one that involves learning to view the world from multiple perspectives as well as shared responsibility for making decisions.

WHAT WENT WRONG?

A strong system of control and accountability—the chain of command—was part of division of labor. The main advantage of division of labor was that people could be trained quickly in one or

17

two processes. Doing a single thing repetitively was supposed to make a person better and faster at the task. Everyone was accountable through a bureaucratic system.

This system has shaped the structure of management and performance within American businesses since 1776. A person could go to work for a company in his twenties and gradually be promoted to perhaps a vice presidency with a corner office. This was the model for all business, whether it was factories, stores, utilities, or design firms. Division of labor reduced the cost of goods. Technology improved production and took over many repetitive tasks.

There were built-in disadvantages as well as advantages to this system. As instructions filtered down the chain of command, errors could occur at each level. Because no one saw the whole picture, and each area understood only its own function, the errors weren't recognized until the end. It would have been less expensive to fix them earlier in the process.

Over the years, production became systematized so one person could do many things; we didn't need as much management. Mergers and acquisitions, combining company structures, was another attempt to decrease administrative costs. The belief was that the processes learned in one field would apply to all, and that one executive could head several types of companies.

Mergers and acquisitions were tried in the home furnishings and design industry. However, in our field, and especially in furniture manufacturing, merger mania, leveraged buy-outs and conglomerates destroyed a lot of companies. Our industry has its own language and specialized processes.

Many changes in our industry are the result of a natural cycle. The businesses that helped shaped the home furnishings and design industry began just after World War II. When these people reached retirement age, they sold their businesses to get the best financial return.

Those who bought the businesses brought financial strength, not knowledge of the industry, with them. Money without knowledge of the industry is just one reason for the chaos in our industry right now.

SEARCHING FOR AN ANSWER

Books on new theories of business management began to appear in the late 1980s: benchmarking, liberation management, I-Power, Total Quality Management, Servant-Leader, and reengineering. What they have in common is an emphasis on communication, respect, applied intelligence, and teamwork. They all eliminate layers of supervisors. The biggest change is in the value system.

Reengineering the Corporation tells us to ignore what is and concentrate on what could be. Reengineering, as authors Hammer and Champy describe it, is "the fundamental rethinking and radical redesign of the business process to achieve dramatic improvements in critical contemporary measures of performance, such as costs, quality, service and speed."

Total Quality Management (TQM) is a popular management theory dedicated to improving the present process. Reengineering asks the question, "Is the present process worth saving?" This is the question many corporations faced in the late 1980s, and the result was downsizing and decentralization into smaller, more independent entities. For some, the current process was not worth saving in its entirety.

Leadership consultant Joe Batten makes the point that TQM as it is currently practiced often is rigid and does not involve the entire organization.

Employee suggestion programs build a sense of community. I-Power, a program based on employee suggestions, concentrates on small changes that can be made by individuals. The office furniture firm of Haworth saved the company an estimated $8.2 million based on 13,000 ideas from employees in 1993.

Open-space meetings are a version of management by team. Anyone with a passion about any company-related issue writes that issue at the top of a large piece of paper and tacks it to the bulletin board in the meeting space. Other people then sign up for a discussion group about it. In each discussion group, the chairs are laid out in a circle. A one-day session lays the groundwork for interdepartmental communication. A three-day meeting is needed when the company wants employees to form groups to carry out their ideas.

THE VALUE OF PEOPLE

Today the value of companies is the value of people, not the building or the price of the equipment. These people sell, they design, they manufacture, and they provide services. If a company is not doing as well as it could, it is probably because it is not doing one of these things as well as it could.

Businesses need to ask basic questions: What really works? What does the client want? How can we eliminate waste and work that doesn't add value?

Many traditional jobs have become simplified to the point where technology does most of the work faster and more accurately. The job of bookkeeper was once a very important position and generally took a full-time employee in even a small firm. The work is now done in a few hours and very often by those who are actually working on the project. Now we have more accountability for a lot less effort.

Today task-oriented jobs are obsolete at many firms. The new system works around a process. The best model I can give you for this business concept is a design project. Look at a project as if one person were going to do the entire thing. This eliminates all of the communication processes. Then consider how to incorporate technology and makes use of the multi-talented people in the firm.

American workers are better than you think. Among the industrial powers, the productivity of the American worker is 30 percent higher than that of his or her Japanese counterpart. And we are increasingly better educated. In 1952, over half the workforce hadn't made it through high school. In 1993, only 13 percent hadn't graduated. More than a quarter of the workforce has a college degree, up from 7.9 percent in 1952.

TODAY'S BUSINESS

Today's business is different. The prevailing mood of the 1990s is to make companies lean, responsive, competitive, efficient, and innovative. Big business was based on economies of scale. Small companies can move quickly; big business has tried to become more like small companies. As a result companies have become smaller and more independent. Many people no longer work for a salary but are consultants or part-time employees. An estimated 41 million Americans now do some work at home.

The market for office design, which made up a large percentage of our business in the 1980s, has shrunk. The office design market is no longer multiple floors of desks, chairs, and landscape cubicles. Equipment takes up less room. Even when we house as many people, the square footage is less. And there is an emerging market for one- and two-person home offices or shared offices. Now people carry office equipment in cars and briefcases.

These smaller companies, when they need design services, need and expect quick response time. Outfitting home offices is a growing specialty. Georgene Pujit, a designer in the New York/New Jersey area, has made home office design her specialty. Her card reads: "we will maximize the image, comfort and efficiency of your home office."

NEW WORK STYLES

Allowing people to do their best work means designing work spaces that take advantage of natural human inclinations.

The office space of the future will be designed for flexibility, for constantly changing groups of two and three as the process demands. This is not a new concept; it has been around since the late 1960s.

With personal computers, modems, and faxes that fit in briefcases, people can work anywhere they happen to be. Technophiles are calling this telecommuting and the "virtual workplace," a take-off on virtual reality.

Jay Chiat, president of the 400-person advertising agency Chiat/Day, compares traditional offices to kindergarten where only two hours of work are done per day. Chiat says he gives his staff the freedom to be more creative and more responsive to clients. Employees work out of their homes or in the offices of the client. Chiat supplies employees with a personal computer, a dedicated telephone line and some furniture. He feels this "virtual agency" will elevate the quality of work his agency produces.

In Manhattan, the 275-member accounting firm of Ernst & Young has devoted one floor to the "officeless" office—cubicles whose would-be occupants must make a reservation to use the space. The concierge keeps employee profiles with preferred offices and floor locations. Within 15 minutes of reserving a space, the employee's nameplate goes up outside the cubicle, his phone number is assigned, and files are placed on his desk. The majority of Ernst & Young consultants have traditional offices, but this setup encourages people who should be doing most of their work on the road to get out on the road.

What is good for one isn't necessarily good for all. Some people become more autonomous and love working without being tied to an office. Others hate it and move to another structure.

A handful of companies hotel their office and cubicle space, Chiat/Day and IBM among them. It does decrease real estate costs—sometimes in half—but critics say it merely underscores the impermanence of the employer/employee relationship. Charles O'Reilly, a professor at Stanford University's graduate school of business, says, "You're sending some very clear signals to people that they're simply an extension of some sort of machine."

Magazines call people who carry their offices in a briefcase "road warriors." Hoteliers have begun to cater to the business traveller, offering functional desks, in-room fax machines, dataports, and dual phone lines.

Hyatt Hotels Business Plan rooms have enhanced lighting, fax machines, two phones, and a custom-designed desk lamp with a power receptacle in the base so business travelers don't have to fumble behind furniture to plug in their laptop computers. Hilton and Radisson offer similar plans. All hoteliers stress the availability of dataport-equipped phones and curtailed phone charges for modem users. All of this comes at a surcharge of about $10-$20 above daily room rate, but rates vary according to location.

The rise in home-based businesses spells opportunity to some real estate developers. A Chicago apartment complex, ParkShore, joined with software developer LaSalle Technical Development to create a 1,300-square-foot executive office center in an upscale apartment building. Tenants have access to a conference room, four networked workstations, and a range of software and platforms. A desktop publishing technician is available at $40 per hour.

The downside to having the technical facilities to be able to work anytime and any place is that some people work 50- to 60-hour weeks. This may be because they have the equipment with them and a free moment, or that they are simply unable to disengage from working, not that employers demand these hours.

In the 1970s, futurists told us that computers meant we would have paperless offices; this simply isn't true. What is true is that personal computers have changed the workplace. In the 1980s, thinking about office design changed because the personal computers were standard equipment. Today in stock brokerages and newspaper offices, there are desks with four and five keyboards and computer screens. Some highly productive employees have no assigned desks at all, and facility managers have become concierges to facilitate the hoteling of desk space.

Technology and knowledge empowered people to make faster, more informed decisions. Companies need fewer people, but the people they have must be smarter and more independent. Workplace design is more flexible and less prescriptive. Small businesses can compete with large ones on a more equal footing. Many of these are positive trends, putting the emphasis on people. These changes are opportunities.

If we do not grasp change by the hand, it will grasp us by the throat.
WINSTON CHURCHILL

4

REALITY CHECK
Industry

The mystique that surrounds the home furnishings and design industry was once an asset, but recent research indicates that consumers are confused by the easy access to products and overloaded with undifferentiated information. What appeared to be mystique is regarded as an elitist attitude, and it works against us now.

To continue making a contribution to the world, we have to make the field more user-friendly.

AN INDUSTRY IN CHAOS

In 1994, 25 percent of all the furniture manufacturers and retailers in America felt the industry was in serious trouble. That is twice the number who felt that way five years ago. If nothing changes, at this pace the industry pessimists will outnumber the optimists in another five years.

That we are in trouble may be the only thing the industry agrees on. The home furnishings and design industry is made up of literally hundreds of crafts, each with its own language and standards, and, as one industry observer commented, it is the only industry in which the branches don't share information. In general, our industry tends to treat information as proprietary. We don't work together.

Many problems can be traced to lack of communication. Manufacturers don't seem to be producing what consumers want to buy. For the past eight years consumers have been telling the industry they want to spend less on furniture. The industry continues to stress construction, and people buy for a combination of rational and emotional reasons. Consumers expect a sofa to last only 8.3 years, according to America's Research Group.

Marketing forecasters say that there has never been a better market for American innovation than right now: good design is salable. On the other hand, only a few design stars have been called on to design mass-produced items for the home market. And star designers are not necessarily the most qualified to design products for general use.

We need fewer and better chosen pieces. Sometimes lines are entirely too broad. We don't need 42 different beiges in one quality of carpet. We do need carpets that go with the latest fabric collections now, not two years later. Even companies that produce both fabric and carpet have this frustrating production lag. When clients are excited about a new color scheme, we want to be able to show them a range of coordinated products, and this is more than a swatch of fabric with smaller swatches attached.

Manufacturers in the contract industry began coordinating colors throughout diverse product lines a few years ago. This shared information gave us laminates, metal finishes, carpets, fabrics—a whole range of products—that worked together easily. Not only does this save time for the designer and client, but each product helps sell the next.

Another problem is that product testing is often done after the furniture and furnishings hit the market. Products are tested for safety and durability, but not for consumer acceptance. One appliance manufacturer spent more in 1993 to test a new refrigerator than the entire furniture industry spend on research in the last decade. This has long been a complaint of furniture designers. The vast majority of manufacturers agree that consumer research would help the industry, but most are unwilling to lead the way.

But if, as pollsters claim, appearance is what drives the industry and what makes consumers buy, why should the industry spend money testing products?

We should test products because appearance includes perceived value, and consumers are very conscious of value and quality. Sometimes a manufacturer's perception of value and quality is very different from the client's. Every other product consumers can buy, from automobiles to toasters, has been tested extensively and the manufacturers emphasize it in promotional materials. This is one area where the home furnishings industry has some catching up to do.

An Industry Report Card

In 1990 I asked a group of designers, architects, business managers, and marketing specialists to evaluate how well our resources met our needs and challenges. The categories were product quality, product design, service, speed of production, technical information, concern for the environment, and concern for environmental illness. Rarely did any participant give the industry any grade higher than a mediocre C. And our industry is supposed to stand for quality, service, and innovation!

Overall, quality is not what it should be. Lines seem nicely designed, but too many of the features can go wrong. For product design, the comment was "Too much frosting, not enough cake." Designers called for a return to basics. Grades given for services were C, D, and F—in other words, mediocre to failing. Participants believed that the system for dealing with problems was inadequate.

Speed of production is an area where designers felt manufacturers were doing well, but no one gave any A's. Some participants gave A's for technical information, but were careful to say the grade was not deserved industry-wide.

In the areas of concern for the environment and environmental illness, designers gave the industry failing and almost failing grades. Their comments:

"Little has been done in this country to demonstrate concern for the environment, even in recycling packaging materials."

"We need more information on levels of formaldehyde and other toxins in products."

"While fabrics are labeled for fiber content, there is no indication of which finishes are applied or what chemical components exist."

What Does Business Think of Design?

Tom Peters praised the design industry in his book *In Search of Excellence* ten years ago, citing Herman Miller as a positive example. Recently he wrote that office furniture introductions were boring, boring, boring! and the residential line is not much different. The furnishings and design industry is not providing the new product excitement that the consumer public wants. Change stimulates people to invest money in their interior space rather than in other things. I don't want a fashion line. I want products that show people how to improve the way they live and work.

In the apparel industry, a certain percentage of each line is designed for runway success only; its real purpose is to generate publicity that may cause buyers to rethink the line. Furniture manufacturers used to create a piece or two of "editor bait" each season—prototypes that hinted at the design direction of the company and helped ensure the salability of products before they went into mass production. Although it is true that most prototypes cannot be manufactured as presented, displaying prototypes to the public can help presell them on an idea.

One of the problems in the furniture industry is that we have not introduced enough of the right kinds of new furniture. Products are refined and polished, but is the product needed in the first place? A lot of products are kept around on the off-chance that they will be needed. If it is marginal, it could be eliminated.

What's wrong with our industry? Michael K. Dugan, president of Henredon Furniture Industries, says, "I think one of the most atrocious mistakes we have made is to allow our thinking to lean to the conclusion that 'if it's ugly it will sell, if it's good looking it won't sell.' Good design is salable."

The design consumer wants good design. The reason a lot of furniture is not selling is that it is either ugly or it doesn't work.

Does the furniture industry lack romance? The industry tried to borrow glamour from the apparel industry in the late 1970s with an influx of couture designers. At the same time Terence Conran opened his first stores in the United States, furniture and home furnishings manufacturers became licensees for designers such as Pierre Cardin and Oleg Cassini. In the 1990s we see Ralph Lauren and Laura Ashley.

The industry already had some unsung heroes whose work dealt with actual needs and whose designs sold very well for their manufacturers. If a designer label adds cachet, why not play up the designers who have worked in our industry, who know how to work with the craftsmen, and who are aware of what production machinery can and cannot do?

There is a problem with pricing. List price is no longer a reasonable measure of what users pay for office furniture. What is list, when one manufacturer sold furniture at 81 percent off list?

The other problem with price is that this industry—unlike the auto industry—has not solved the problem of how to produce high quality at low cost. "Every business day sees too many new interior design products coming to market with little to commend except low cost," writes Roger Yee, editor of *Contract Design* magazine. We are producing better products, but that doesn't mean every item is fully tested before it comes to market.

DISTRIBUTION PROBLEMS

Technology has decreased the cost of making products; those that are available are made better and sell for less than ever before. Today distribution can be as much as 85 percent of a product's price. Distribution is defined as every cost—administrative, selling, showroom expenses, taxes, insurance—except the cost of materials and labor.

The future of interior design and furnishings will be based not only on producing quality products at a lower cost, but on finding a less costly method of distribution.

We've lost our distribution structure. There are fewer than 15 percent of the furniture and department stores that there were 15 years ago. The number of office furniture dealers is also eroding. There is a pent-up desire on the part of the consumer for furniture and furnishings, but there are fewer places to see, test, and try new items.

Industry observer Jerry Epperson believes distribution is perhaps the greatest factor in the success of any furniture manufacturer. A principal in the firm Mann, Armistead & Epperson Investment Bankers & Advisers, Epperson says 1994 will be the year of the electronic retailing of furniture.

Today you can buy food, clothing, or furniture quick fast and sloppy, but we have lost the opportunity to learn as we buy. Many times you buy the wrong thing. How many times have you bought something you thought was great but it really didn't work for you? The truth is that if you had understood that in the first place, you probably would not have bought it.

Once upon a time, the retail industry was dedicated to both educating and supplying. A typical furniture store would explain all the advantages of a particular product: how it worked, how to use it, what to do with it, and how to maintain it. As customers learn about a product, we begin to need it and then buy it.

Today furniture stores such as these don't exist. There aren't many opportunities for people to come in and figuratively kick the tires as they would for a new car, no place to test the way the cabinet doors open, to see which chair fits best, to learn that there is a difference between the chair they have at home and the ones they see in magazines and catalogs. There is no place for consumers to learn they have a need.

Are people really buying just to stock yard sales? This was not the way we bought years ago. Whether it was clothing or furnishings, we bought things to last. We also expected and got education and service. Retail stores had long-term employees who knew their customers. We went in two or three times a year to purchase clothing, and the salespeople would see that all the items were properly coordinated. In old-style furniture stores and design studios, the interior designer helped you select furniture that worked together. It didn't matter that it might take years to finish the home. If you had a problem with a product even eight years after you bought it, there was a system to take care of it.

Since producing quality items is so much less expensive today, many products that a few years ago were available only through interior designers and architects are in the general market at less than we could sell them for. This gives the consumer the illusion that designers are no longer needed. They feel that with the lower price, they can afford to make a mistake. The disparity in pricing gives consumers the impression that price is the main issue in whether to buy. The industry must refocus the consumer's attention on other factors.

Where Can Consumers Test Products?

Consumers are not learning about new products that are part of the interior design vocabulary today. They are using products incorrectly. This diminishes the value of the product and can poison their perception of the manufacturer. Consumers are losing the opportunity to live with and enjoy many of the things that the furnishing and design industry can offer.

Industry surveys today tell us that consumers want information and the return of the knowledgeable salesperson or designer. There is an unlimited demand for products and design services, and experience supports my belief. We have all designed rooms for ourselves that we thought were great, until the next furniture market when we saw a new product that fit even better into our present way of life, or was a better quality. Once a client has a chair that really fits and is made of quality materials, he or she wants that particular product—not the older, lower quality item. They have learned that there is a difference.

People need to experience design products. Electronic retailing is being tested by parts of the home furnishings industry. I don't think showing a product and talking about it on the Home Shopping Network or other shopping shows is enough. Television doesn't let you touch a fabric or walk through a space. Department and furniture stores used to let you walk in and feel that you were in a room in a home. There were beautiful examples, such as set-ups of full kitchens with people cooking in them. But these types of department and furniture stores are decreasing.

To sell design products, we need to present them well. Catalogs, television, and computer screens aren't enough because they don't provide enough of the tactile and the experiential aspects. You cannot sit on a chair at the same time you see it on television or a computer screen.

The furnishings and design industry has products that cannot be sold well in newspapers or on television. Furniture, fabrics, carpets, and accessories must be touched, felt, sat in, and experienced. Seeing a picture of a room and actually being in it are quite different experiences. Walt Disney said that we must deal with all the senses. And interior design takes in all of them. Our challenge is to educate people today.

Today, outfitting a room is not a user-friendly experience. Consumers go to a bed and bath store for sheets and towels, a plumbing supply for fixtures, a lighting store for lamps and lighting—a different store for each new item. What consumers want is a vision of the total environment, and this calls for a change in merchandising. Furniture retailers don't normally carry home furnishings accessories; this is viewed as competitive and is more labor intensive than simply putting in another piece of furniture.

In response to consumer demand, some furniture retailers have begun to sell accessories as well. Typically, accessories in furniture stores were not sold until the vignette was dismantled. This has begun to change; restockable coordinated accessories programs are now offered to retail stores. The Waverly Place environment is a merchandising concept that helps retailers present a coordinated design environment of fabrics, wallcoverings, window treatments, bed coverings, and decorative pillows and accessories in a small amount of showroom space. Furniture retailers say it gives people a custom look without the custom price. It is instant gratification. The collection requires a minimum of 700 square feet.

What Business Are We In?

The industry is attacking the distribution problem on several fronts. Design centers, traditionally to-the-trade only, have begun to open their doors to the public. This alienates interior designers and architects, who see this as direct competition.

Design centers and their tenants must decide what business they are in: wholesale or retail. Tenants of design centers are in the business of selling wholesale. They are used to conveying information at the designer level, generally more complex than that of the consumer because designers are educated to ask specific questions and specify furniture all the time as opposed to every five years or so.

For design centers to deal directly with the public demands a different orientation. It isn't enough just to show a chair; the chair must be shown in a setting to demonstrate its relationship to other products. Many design centers presently show completed rooms such as kitchens, bedrooms, and living rooms. This is perfect for the consumer, but it isn't enough. Sales people and sales training must also be geared to the consumer.

With wholesale, it is understood that another person or group will handle the direct retail education and customer service. In retail, the retailer handles service and communication with the end user. This is everything from presenting products to the client in their own language (not designer language), delivery and the manner of delivering products, on through repairs and problems for the next few years.

Many products in design centers are created for experienced designers. They are not easy to use, but special and unusual. Putting home furnishings and design products in the wrong places, using them incorrectly, or representing them as doing things they will not do well is bad for the manufacturer and the designer. If a very delicate chair is placed where it gets heavy use, it will be destroyed. Using good products inappropriately hurts the entire design industry.

Someone has to make the judgments of what belongs where. This is the traditional role of the designer, and this responsibility should rest with the designer. Designers have both the scientific and the artistic backgrounds to judge where a piece should or should not be used. When design centers sell directly to the public, who makes that judgement? Selling directly to consumers entails the responsibilities of visiting the location, as designers do, observing the ways people use furniture, and passing judgment on the correct application of products.

When the product is delivered and needs repair, who takes care of it? For design centers to deal responsibly with consumers, they need service departments, facilities to follow through on and maintain the furniture and furnishings they sell.

Consumers who have dealt directly with the manufacturer through 800 telephone numbers know that they don't have follow-up services, and have in effect given this up for lower prices. The sad part is so often a good piece of furniture that is damaged or has simple problems does not get repaired because there is no vehicle in place to take care of it.

The Dallas Design District has invested nearly $2 million in developing a building to communicate the design experience. This is great! This is part of future consumer education. However, it is not enough. Design centers that sell direct to the consumer are doing themselves and the manufacturers a disservice. Manufacturers and designers both need to understand that full service should be available; that buying furniture without a specification is like buying medicine without a prescription. Consumers realize that they are buying furniture without a safety net, but see no alternative.

Reaching Out

The Atlanta Decorative Center developed a six-part series for Georgia Public television. The Design Center of the Americas (DCOTA) in Dania, Florida, reserved national air time for a series in late 1994. Both programs emphasize why using an interior designer and a design center will make the most of a client's investment.

In Dallas, the Design Experience, a 15,000-square-foot multimedia consumer education center includes a 7500-square-foot gallery, a theater for seminars and video presentations, and a studio featuring a touch computer screen that allows the user to access a referral roster of member designers and architects and images of their work, a style guide, and a product locator. Designers resent the purchasing service that allows consumers to buy at a discount from the showroom or sample store.

At least one design center management does not want to give consumers the ability to purchase directly from design centers. Christopher Kennedy, executive vice president of Merchandise Mart Properties, (which manages the Merchandise Mart in Chicago, the D & D Building in New York, and the Washington Design Center in Washington, D.C.) says the answer lies in viewing the consumer, rather than architects and designers, as the ultimate client in the distribution channel. This means strengthening the position of designers and architects as non-stocking dealers to replace diminishing retail sources.

Changing Directions

The office furniture industry seems to have been caught flat-footed by the fact that business needs less, not more, office space due to downsizing and the change to team style management. Some manufacturers are trying to combat the problem by offering deep discounts. Others have finally taken the advice of their office dealers and offer lower-cost furniture, but they are offering it directly to consumers, cutting out the dealers.

The change to collaborative management is the death knell of the cubicle. Businesses now want "enterprise" furniture, not just to accommodate a new management style but to deal with existing physical facilities in ways manufacturers never dreamed of. The president of Steelcase challenged his people to come up with different ways to help the clients. Haworth has a room of test products: among them the office/locker, for people who share office space, and the office in a cubicle, for rental at transit centers.

In the office industry, firms that stick to making and selling office furniture as we know it are likely to become obsolete by current management styles.

The home furnishings industry foresaw that more people would be working at home, and began producing home office furniture in the late 1980s. It has also moved into niche marketing, recognizing people's differences after years of making products to fit the common denominator—the fast-food approach. There are furnishings for a romantic mood, for rough-and-ready living, nostalgia, Mission, Victorian, or any style of life a person wants and needs.

"New Retailers," so-called by *Metropolitan Home* magazine, are bringing high–end furniture out from behind the closed doors of design centers. For these retail pioneers, furniture is the new fashion and style is what they want. They stock modern classics from manufacturers such as Driade, Atelier International, Pace Collection, Dux of Sweden, Disform of Spain, B&B Italia, and Artemide, as well as art furniture. Some offer volume discounts. And entrepreneurial interior designers are opening retail outlets, making designer-quality merchandise accessible to those who don't need professional help to furnish their homes.

Furniture now comes in sizes. Short and very tall people no longer have to make do with furniture designed to fit the moderately tall. It also comes with a choice of seat depths and cushion densities to accommodate a variety of seating preferences.

There are wonderful products available to those who know about them. A lot of needs are going unrecognized at the moment. Many products could be used more broadly with minor changes. There is the technical knowledge to make other items for which a consumer need has been expressed, but the items have not gone into production. The industry must take stock of what exists and what can be sold.

Distribution is a challenge: delivering the right product in the right manner to the right people at the right price. Clients relate to people, and people demonstrate the products.

5

REALITY CHECK
Trends and the Design World

Running a design business today without tracking the trends is like designing an apartment for a person you've never met and know nothing about. It's possible, but it's a lot harder than it has to be.

Being a news junkie or reading four newspapers a day doesn't guarantee you are aware of all the events that affect the design industry. You can't rely on the late-night news to tell you everything you need to know. You have to combine knowledge of client demands and industry involvement. A pioneer trend tracker and author of *Trend Tracking* (John Wiley, 1990), Gerald Celente suggests that if you read only one newspaper a week, read Saturday's, because it has the most vital information of the week. Saturday's paper is smaller and will feature weekend statements about business. Because the news is read after the stock market closes, businesses time press releases for the weekend in the hope that by Monday things will have lost their impact. Newspapers often run articles on trends in weekend editions.

SPOTTING A TREND

A trend is a predictable sequence of events, says Celente. "You need at least two points to plot a direction. At first you won't know if what you're seeing is a trend or not." A trend meets three other conditions: it has social, economic and political significance. If the effects are trivial, or it has only political importance, it's not a trend.

Trend watchers such as Celente and Ken Dychtwald, president of Age Wave Inc., suggest you keep trend files with very broad categories. *Home Office Computing* magazine gives as an example homelessness, one of the fastest growing categories. They place that in the category of family, which has effects on the categories of

---

Other Trends

- Appearance, not construction, drives the furniture industry.

  SOURCE: AMERICA'S RESEARCH GROUP

- Small businesses that employ fewer than 100 people are creating jobs faster than larger businesses.

  SOURCE: RUKEYSER

- The information superhighway is an as-yet nonexistent network of cable and telephone lines that will deliver vast new amounts of information directly to consumer's homes.

  SOURCE: *MODERN MATURITY*

- Word-of-mouth accounts for at least 67 percent of designer referrals.

  SOURCE: AMERICA'S RESEARCH GROUP

- Percentage of interior designers who would not support a showroom that allowed direct consumer purchases: 86.5.

  SOURCE: AMERICAN SOCIETY OF INTERIOR DESIGNERS

- Mail-order sales of home furnishings accessories reached $1.45 billion in 1992, and this accounts for only 4 percent of retail purchases.

  SOURCE: *ACCESSORY MERCHANDISING*

- Percentage of buildings with chronic indoor air quality problems: 40.

  SOURCE: WORLD HEALTH ORGANIZATION

politics, health, and the economy. The key to a good trend-tracking system is connections between fields.

Trend-tracking is something you will have to do for yourself, Celente cautions. Having someone else do it is like having someone exercise for you.

Finally, maintain a sense of proportion and don't get too far ahead of your market, because, as Celente says, most of America looks more like Roseanne than Murphy Brown. "You can't make money as an entrepreneur 20 years ahead," says Dychtwald. "You have to be two years ahead."

In the 1970s, when Saphier Lerner Schindler became SLS Environetics and developed computer programs that enabled its architects and designers to design on the mainframe computer, individual designers regarded it as a tool for gargantuan design firms. Today there is similar software for personal computers, and it is so simple that it is marketed to consumers.

SLS Environetics invested in their future, predicted a need, and probably created a demand, but the process was so complex that it took two years to train their own architects to use the tool. The firm's principals predicted that someday every designer would use computers as a design tool. A lot of us thought they were dreaming, and just as off the wall as the futurists who, in the early 1970s, predicted paperless offices.

Manufacturers of residential furniture targeted the home office in the late 1980s, producing office furnishings to complement various home decors. Interior designers and contract furniture manufacturers did not take it seriously enough. Some office dealers did, but their requests for a quick delivery, low-cost line were ignored until recently. Home offices are a major growth area today.

What consumers are looking for in the near future are the same products and services they want today. If they had the information, they would want more.

RECOGNIZING A PATTERN

How do you recognize an event of global significance? It's not always readily apparent. Desert Storm showed us that the age of high technology is here, not coming. This war was fought with computers. Computers, modems, and satellite receivers mean easy access to knowledge. War wasn't the dynamic change. It was the graphic demonstration of the strength that rapid communications brings to a venture. We can't ignore computers any more. We must accommodate computers in the spaces we design and if we personally don't use them in our work, our competitors will.

Trends can start small. "The Boy in the Plastic Bubble" started as a news item about a child born without a functioning immune system and it led to a 1976 movie loosely based on fact. Twenty years later, we've learned that prolonged exposure to some chemicals can weaken the entire immune system, and everyone has come into contact with airborne toxins.

Air quality is a consciousness-raising issue. It put a hotel in Philadelphia out of business due to an airborne bacterium now called *Legionella*. Concern for air quality has led to laws on public smoking. Sick building syndrome puts every product that goes into a building under scrutiny, from the adhesives used to lay carpets to the fabric finishes, to the composition of furniture and paints, as well as the products used for maintenance.

This adds a new factor to the interior design mix. We have to deal with visible and invisible issues. An environment should function well for its inhabitants, it should look good, and if it doesn't actively support good health, at least it doesn't poison the people who live in it. It's no longer enough to generally know how furniture is constructed. We also have to know which components are likely to cause trouble when they come in contact with common substances.

Our consciousness has been raised about air quality. The main worry is no longer whether the furniture produces toxic gases in a fire, but what common business and residential products contaminate our air. I cannot help but wonder how many currently standard items will someday be proven sources of serious contaminants. And because as designers we specified many of them, you can bet that we will be considered responsible.

You don't immediately know that a specific event signals a dynamic change that will affect business. A blaring headline or a long story on the nightly news doesn't necessarily signal the kind of change that will affect the way you do business. It may take a month or two to build significance, or it may take several years. An event that was a throwaway news item at first could turn out to have been the starting point for a world-shaking change, but you'd never know it unless you had a basis for comparison. That's why you can't read one newspaper a month and half-listen to the nightly news and expect to be well-informed.

FIVE TRENDS

Already in the 1990s several trends are emerging. The **computer** has gone from a tool of big business to a **communication necessity** that is easy to use and the core of any information system. Anyone can use it; you don't have to be an expert. Computers have changed the services we can sell. It may be hard to sell space planning since Steelcase will send CAD-drawn plans in 24 hours if given the right information.

The breakup of big business is a second trend. Hammer and Champy's *Reengineering the Corporation* is a best-selling book on restructuring companies, but it didn't spark the trend. It only reports how to manage this change. And this change is an opportunity for the interior design and furnishings industry to restructure the interiors of these downsized companies.

In the interior design industry, I think we knew before other industries that you can get only so big before the system starts working against you and quick changes become impossible. We saw it in the 1970s, when Burlington bought Stendig and other furniture firms and within a very few years sold them. A lot of family-owned furniture businesses were bought by corporations that sold the businesses back to the families or to the workers, often within two years.

Large corporations were unsuccessful in operating furniture factories because they thought these companies were just like their other companies. But furniture requires craftsmanship and attention to fine details. This was foreign to the way most corporations were run, and too difficult to incorporate into their operating procedures. And furniture is a customer-driven industry. In the 1970s and 1980s, amassing size to get power was the name of the game. In the 1990s, flexibility is the key.

Today there is growth in small firms that supply specialty items, in part an answer to the backlash against mass production, a backlash John Naisbitt termed "high touch." At the International Contemporary Furniture Fair in Javits Center in May of 1994, hundreds of small craftsmen were producing and selling their own special items. Only a few of our usual resources presented products.

At the same time, the number of suppliers steadily dwindled as more and more processes were automated.

The third trend is that **people are looking at lifestyle rather than career**. In the 1950s Dad could give his all to his business and the family would survive because Mom took care of the practicalities of life. In the 1970s women tried to "have it all" by working at careers rather than jobs, and then coming home to another full day's work at maintaining the home. By the 1980s women realized that having it all was not possible if you had to do it all by yourself.

Today it's acceptable for men to play very strong, even dominant, roles in child-rearing. It's acceptable for women to choose to be mother only, professional only, or both—with special concessions. Some men have discovered that there is a satisfaction in sharing the chores of nurturing and cooking and housekeeping. Not only that, but the physical acts involved in housekeeping are a natural antidote to the stresses of the workplace. If you can make it as a family, you also have the skills to make it in business.

So we have a change in values. It's no longer enough to have a great career. It has to be balanced by health-related personal enrichment, family life, and family activity. Corporations have discovered that where this balance exists, fewer executives are forced to take advantage of corporate mental health and addiction programs.

There is a grass-roots change in lifestyle and the way people work. There is a move toward group living: two or more families or single parents share living quarters, generally a house. They also share housekeeping and nurturing responsibilities. In Mendocino

County, California, a group of friends built a living compound currently used as shared vacation space but designed with retirement and senior living in mind.

The fourth trend is that **the economy is not growing for the individual.** Standards of living are dropping or stagnating. Of course this is in part a direct result of the third trend, not spending every waking hour devoted to working and earning money. And in part it is just that it is harder than ever to earn above minimum wage, because that is the only part of the national employment picture that is growing. With corporate downsizing, middle and upper management are forced out, and the remaining people work longer hours for the same or less pay.

The fifth trend is a **return to working at home.** Many people who were forced out of or elected to leave staff positions now work as independent contractors. Some jobs are arranged so the employee may only spend three days a week in the office, working from home the other two days. And retirees no longer stop working completely. Many start new businesses or remain in the workforce as independent contractors and consultants, both paid and volunteer. All of them need business-related space in the home.

Computers, high technology telephone lines, and a change in business attitudes have made working at home possible. It is cottage industry.

Five Trends of This Decade

1. The computer has gone from a tool of big business to a communication necessity that is easy to use and the core of any information system

2. Breakup of big business/strengthening and growth of smaller firms

3. People are looking at lifestyle rather than career

4. The economy is not growing for the individual

5. A return to working at home

IT'S NOT THE TREND, IT'S THE REACTION

So much of our thinking is manipulated by futurists and prophets with the ear of the media. A representative of the Club of Rome spoke at NEOCON in the early 1970s, predicting that in 40 years the world's supply of oil would be depleted. In 1973 and 1977 we had oil shortages and long lines at service stations.

It is twenty years later. By the Club of Rome's timetable based on the technology of the time, we should have 15 or 16 years worth of oil left. But today, there are over 90 years of oil left. The prediction in the 1970s was based on then current technology and standards. Drilling techniques have improved; oil wells are dug deeper; and the oil in Alaska has become accessible through the Alaskan pipeline. Gasoline use has been reduced by approximately 50 percent, buildings are better insulated, and other fuel use has become more efficient.

I am sure the Club of Rome's prediction was overstatement. If we use predictions of disaster as a reason for change, that is much less wasteful and more constructive than panic-rationing of resources.

Throughout history there have been fears of shortages. In the 1800s fear of a whale oil shortage caused an international panic because everyone was afraid they would have no oil for their lanterns. But in 1859 fossil oil was discovered in Pennsylvania. Before that, the British government had thought that England would be finished by the end of the 1800s because they would be out of coal. By the end of the 1800s Britain was using fossil oil and the British government is still operational.

The world economic system affects the interior furnishings industry. For example, silk was once very expensive, but changes in the world market have brought the price down. At one time we had in our studio a silk rug worth $85,000. Ten years later the same rug was worth about $35,000. The rug had not changed; the difference was China was open and now we have a lot of silk. Whether it is silk carpets or clothing, we are buying silk products for a lot less money than ever before.

The world is full of resources, whether we use them or not. Technology and politics help determine availability. Russia has more raw materials than any other country in the world but it does not have the technology and is unable to use what it has. At one time most products, including furniture, were very expensive to produce; at least 50 percent of the retail price was production costs. Today the cost of production is about 15 percent of the retail price.

In the movie *The Graduate* (1967), Dustin Hoffman's character asked his girlfriend's father what he should do to be successful. "Plastics," he was told, and it was funny at the time. Now we can't imagine living without plastics. It's hard to say what we should go into today because things change so quickly.

How many things have you bought in the past year for your own use that did not exist 20 years ago? Not many. In the furnishings and design industry, there are wonderful products that our clients don't know they need or how to ask for because they don't know they exist.

TECHNOLOGY

Technology has changed the way we work, the way we think, and our perception of history. It has taken over a lot of the repetitive work that absorbed so much office time and permits design offices to spend more time and energy on the creative aspects of our business. It has even caused spelling changes. The Spanish language has eliminated two letters from its alphabet to become more computer-friendly.

What Do You Know?

Modern technology is proving many "facts" to be incorrect. Paint chips and wallpaper scraps from historic houses were analyzed, giving us a truer picture of the colors that were used in those eras. If you are a historian, you can't rely solely on your old favorite history books: Nutting, Sherrill Whiton, the bibles of the industry.

Technology doesn't just rewrite history, it also adds information. For Knoll's Parachute Chair, a hundred people of different sizes and occupations sat on electronic sensor mats to measure how weight is distributed across a chair's seat and back. The pressure "maps" were used to shape the chair and adjust its foam to reduce pressure hot spots.

Through technology, we are bringing expert information and materials to our clients and to our staff for every portion of the project, from selling to the smallest detail. Through videos, we can have experts on call to demonstrate how a piece of furniture works. Videos help train us and our staff. Presenting information visually makes communicating our vision easier with the variety of support materials and processes available to us today.

Libraries as Resource Centers

Design libraries used to be stockpiles of sample books and dog-eared catalogs. In an information-hungry age, they are evolving into essential resource centers. First you search through the resource materials in your studio. A design library doesn't replace the design center, but you will have the basics from the companies you have worked with and the products you trust.

Still, a library is only as good as the resources it contains. While you can rely on manufacturer's representatives to supply you with literature and product samples, many design firms find that evaluating a product before putting it into the library results in a leaner, meaner library of resources you are confident in. Meyer Associates in Ardmore, Pennsylvania, also reevaluates its resource center yearly to ensure that only quality products make the final cut.

Can you find what you need? Many firms organize the library by major categories such as health care, corporate offices, residential, and so on, and by price point within the category. Large firms such as the Callison Partnership in Seattle hold library-sponsored seminars and forums. Environmentally friendly products and practices was a recent topic.

Although most of the material is printed media, some material takes advantage of the latest in electronic technology. The Construction/Specification Institute has a microfilm/microfiche program. McGraw Hill's electronic CAP-Sweets software and Eclat's CD-ROM disk technology are designed to put information in the hands of designers quickly. However, nothing replaces the actual hard samples. For that reason, we still have a paper-based library.

A computer, a modem, and a bulletin board system are your ticket to the information resources of libraries around the world. The Internet network provides access to the on-line catalogs of public and academic libraries, but it is not all free. Public libraries do not charge for using on-line catalogs, and university libraries are usually open to the public, although some do have fees for some services, such as access to the Internet. You often must pay for printouts, although printouts of the abstracts may be free of charge.

Technology That Changes the Way People Work

Information technologies mean huge changes. They make team efforts easier to control and fewer layers of organization are required. Retailing giants such as Wal-Mart and Kmart couldn't operate without computers, databases, and computer networks. Information technology means small businesses can compete with larger ones on a fairly even footing.

Telephone companies offer access to the information super-highway in two ways: Integrated Services Digital Network (ISDN) and fiber optics. ISDN works on old-fashioned copper telephone lines but can handle simultaneous voice and data transactions. Data transfers are fast, up to ten times the speed of the 14,400 modem. By 1995, ISDN will be available in most of the United States, but it costs about $150 to install and $27 to $97 per month. (These figures were accurate in early 1994.) Fiber optics, a more reliable phone line, is as yet unavailable unless you are in a major metropolitan area or a densely populated region, but that changes almost daily. Databases take the place of physical files; we can search through more information more quickly than when all our information was on paper. Computerized databases can lead you to specialized journals and statistics on just about every subject. The services have articles ready to print, as well as short abstracts.

Tech-friendly law firms perform legal research on-line and with data on CD-ROM, making the law library largely for show. It would be useful for the furnishings and design industry to have building codes and other reference material on CD-ROM. Very few programs for the architecture and design industry are available in this format as yet.

Technology means we need different kinds of people working with us. We can't afford task-specialized employees. We need people who can not only process words, but who can shape the data and make some decisions. For our clients, this has meant a decrease in secretarial space because the PC is standard office equipment in every office from CEO to junior assistant.

Industry-specific software can save a lot of time. Like bookkeeping, specifying is demanding, essential, complex, and repetitive. The specification systems of the American Institute of Architects (AIA) and the Construction Sciences Research Foundation (CSRF) have been worked into a high-level set of WordPerfect macro programs, Masterworks, and MicroComspec. As of July 1994, the programming firm, Arcom planned to do a version for WordPerfect for Windows, and is looking into the possibility of reworking the macros for other word processing systems.

CAD and Virtual Reality

Where once a designer's vision of a project was communicated to clients through verbal skills and perhaps a rendering, we now have CAD and virtual reality to help convey the potential. These tools have become increasingly necessary. CAD is nowhere near as complicated to learn as it used to be. CAD is moving into consumer applications ranging in price from $14.95 for Expert Home Design in the DOS format to Macinteriors at $129 in the Macintosh format. Once a program is deemed ready for the consumer market, it is fairly user-friendly. Professional quality CAD programs now cost about a tenth of their original prices, in the hundreds of dollars rather than in the thousands. Windows-based CAD and Mac software allow you to drag and drop furnishings from libraries of symbols programs into your drawings, a great time-saver.

The advantage of CAD is not that it takes less time to make an initial drawing. It doesn't. It's that once you have the initial drawing, changes are so much simpler to make and more accurate than redrawing everything by hand. As with everything else done by computer, there is a substantial investment in time to learn the application. If you are really good at CAD and sure of yourself, your client might enjoy watching you make some of the simpler changes on screen.

Our resources have invested in proprietary software, both for the planning and programming stages of projects and to provide almost point-of-purchase renderings. Kitchen cabinet manufacturers have proprietary computer software that lets them show prospective buyers the way their kitchens will look within minutes, as opposed to several days or a week for a rendering. In the office furniture industry, similar software helps dealer reps to determine for clients on-site their space planning requirements, including the necessary number of work stations.

Virtual reality, interactive computer simulations, allow designers and clients to "walk" through a space during the design phase when changes are still relatively easy to make. With a wheelchair simulator O'Donnell Wicklund Pigozzi and Peterson Architects discovered that a bathroom countertop was two inches too deep for wheelchair patients to use the sink in a planned 14-room hospital installation. This more than justified the expense of the simulation.

Virtual reality demands an investment of $5,000 to $10,000 (as of April 1994) and a questing spirit or a willingness to play video games. The systems have at least one computer, a visual display and a device for interacting with the computer. A helmet blocks out the user's actual surroundings and presents the visual display. The display image is as crude and fuzzy as images in video games. High resolution systems exist in monochrome, but the cost to anyone other than research labs and the military is astronomical: $200,000. For most of us, simpler virtual reality may become a standard tool.

Change creates stress, and individuals who have to experience new and different things need to adjust their stress levels. It has been argued that certain people may not be able to separate virtual reality, which is a fantasy produced by a computer, from actual reality. They would find this very disturbing. According to clinical psychologist Dr. Arnold Lazarus, however, "This would be true only of people who are already pretty disturbed, like border-line personalities, potential schizophrenics, and fragile egos. Most people will know very clearly what is fantasy and what is reality because they are always aware that they are playing a game."

Experiences with virtual reality can become part of the way we think. We will constantly be using computers and very high tech knowledge bases. This trains us to become smart in the ways of computers, and to differentiate a computer-generated adventure or experience from than a physical one. Probably there will be a synergy of these two kinds of experience, virtual experience and actual experience.

When the automobile was first invented, people said, "We move by walking! How are we going to deal with sitting in a vehicle that moves faster than horses? What will happen to us?" Well, you don't have to do anything. Virtual reality is here, and we will deal with it as it comes up. As with cars, unless we crash, we will adjust.

Some people will love virtual reality and will perform better because it is available as a tool. Below is a listing of 25 new business tools.

New Business Tools

1. Computer-Aided Design—software such as ANSYS, from Swanson Analysis Systems, AutoCAD from Autodesk, and IBM's CATIA permit the user to refine a design without redrawing from scratch for each change.

2. Paperless Manufacturing—products are designed on CAD, digitized, and sent to PCs and other terminals on the factory floor.

New Business Tools (*Continued*)

3. Groupware—a class of products that exchanges information, combining E-mail, networking, and database technologies.

4. Online Service—electronic information services such as Lexis, Nexis, and NewsEdge can cut research time with computer searching.

5. Document Management—a standard generalized markup language (SGML), an international standard for formatting data, allows information to keep its look and feel with different hardware, software, and applications.

6. Customer Service—meeting customer needs is so important that large North American companies are investing in technology that puts data about the customers at their fingertips.

7. Point of Sale Terminals—the scanners which record prices at checkout counters also record whose products are selling well and at what price. This lets retailers use point-of-sale data in day-to-day decisions.

8. Servers—computers that store files and run applications for networks of PCs, or "clients." The server replaces mainframes.

9. Networks—networked PCs are linked by wires to hubs, which permit different kinds of computers to communicate and share data.

10. Databases—database technology organizes information into sets of tables. It allows users to ask questions of data: how many clients have children under college age?

11. Printers—printers can print in color with high resolution, printing color transparencies for presentations and booklets as well as handling text for day-to-day word processing.

12. Voice Recognition—voice recognition software enables users to enter text and numbers into a computer without touching a keyboard. DragonDictate from Dragon Systems in Newton, Massachusetts, and Verbex Listen for Windows from Verbex Voice Systems in Edison, New Jersey, offer this technology.

New Business Tools (*Continued*)

13. Storage Protection—new technologies such as hard-cartridge drives for computers allow users to store large amounts of data to a single location. This is especially useful for networked workstations.

14. Fax Machines—improvements in hardware and software now let you send and receive multiple faxes independent of your work on the computer and eliminate the step of creating hard copy to feed to the fax modem.

15. Scanners—devices that read text from paper and enter it into the computer as digital information.

16. Pen Notebooks—lightweight computers offer 486 technology with pressure-sensitive screens for penned entries and keyboards for keyed entries.

17. Flash Technology—flash memory chips are encased in credit-card-sized plastic packages that slip into computer notebooks and personal digital assistants. Hard to damage, they require about half the energy of a standard hard drive.

18. Advanced Fiber Optics—called the foundation of the information superhighway, fiber optic networks carry voice, data, and images. Most phone systems are still hooked by copper wire.

19. Wireless Technology—cellular phones and pagers are a strong wireless market. Pagers now have liquid crystal display screens which can transmit data.

20. Videoconferencing—participants can hear and see who they are talking to. Desktop videoconferencing also allows them to share data. Software for this can cost anywhere from $100 for a Windows program to $2,000 for a full system that does not includes the cost of new phone lines.

21. Graphics Technology—cordless pens and tablets, more sensitive than keyboard and mouse, give artists greater control over the images they create.

New Business Tools (*Continued*)

22. Data Compression—data and video can be shrunk for storage and transmission and restored to full size for use.

23. Object Orientation—Windows icons and MAC files are objects. Object-oriented programming simplifies changing and creating computer programming.

24. Virtual Reality—three-dimensional animation and computer simulations. The computer game SimCity from Maxis is a simple example. AutoCAD and 3D Studio allow an architectural firm to experience designing buildings without the expense of physical models.

25. Geographic Systems—graphic software systems link maps with other databases. This lets companies do geographic analyses and show the results on a map.

SOURCE: *US News & World Report*

6

REALITY CHECK
Clients

The customer of today is different from the customer in the 1980s. There is less disposable income and a greater demand for value. Time and relationships have become our most valuable commodity. Paradoxically, style matters more than construction, and information is a selling point.

DEMOGRAPHICS

Design clients are most often successful professionals who work 60 to 80 hours a week. In the 1970s these same people might have worked 40 to 50 hours. Not only are they exhausted, these people have very little time and energy to spend on interior design.

Statisticians claim we work an average of a hundred thousand hours in a traditional lifetime, and that this takes 47 years. When people are working 70 hours a week, they accumulate a hundred thousand hours in thirty years. This means designers are dealing with exhausted and burnt-out people. (See Juliette Schor's *The Overworked American*.)

INCOMES CHANGED

Between 1977 and 1989, incomes changed. Almost two-thirds of the nation's income went to 660,000 families, the wealthiest one percent. Their incomes rose 77 percent, from $315,000 to $560,000. This is the group of people who bought and furnished sumptuous homes, purchased design services, and spent money on some of the luxuries of life. During this same period, the income of the middle class rose only 4 percent.

People are working more and earning less. Weekly earnings, adjusted for inflation, are actually 2 percent less than they were in 1959. The percentage of Americans working has increased by 12 percent. Average income per capita has increased, but income per person has dropped.

The middle class was responsible for the growth of interior design since World War II. They may have budgeted or planned their projects a room at a time, but they did a lot for the profession. This built the design business, forming a good base for volume.

Today the middle class has dropped out of our client base. In fact, 40 percent of these people actually ended up with less income than before.

Fewer babies are being born, so we are looking at a future with fewer clients, all of whom are less wealthy than they had been. This makes them extremely discriminating.

THE WAY WE LIVE

Before 1980 I had a lot of clients who came in each year to do a room or a project. This gave us a nice running base. In 1977 to 1978 this started to drop. Our projects were larger and more expensive and involved custom merchandise and original proprietary design. This meant we were not selling merchandise off the floor. We had to change the design of the studio and reduce inventory because the turnover wasn't fast enough.

In the 1980s, home was just a place to change clothes in order to go out again. People went to country clubs, health clubs, restaurants. Their houses were used strictly for sleep and storage. In the 1990s clients need more from their living spaces. People want home to be a safe haven, a retreat. Home is for recreation, rejuvenation, and nurturing. Faith Popcorn's term "cocooning" applies.

People use rooms differently. Kitchens are now the family room, bedrooms are mini-retreats, and outdoor areas are fully incorporated into the usable space of the home, according to Dr. Michael Solomon, chair of the marketing department at Rutgers University and a consultant on consumer behavior. He says that when people buy a new home, they are not just moving but "often buying different living situations and so need furnishings that address these different needs."

An estimated 41 million Americans now do some work at home. There is a need for furniture and design services that make this easier.

Our society measures achievement by consumption. Today *time* is our most precious commodity. The people who purchase design services today have very little time. That is one reason they want our services.

WHAT DO CLIENTS WANT?

Change and novelty are important. Clients may want a traditional item, but they also want to know that it has some characteristics that are different than furniture and furnishings they already own. Otherwise why bother buying it!

Clients want new furniture styles and value style over construction. Consumers seek out resources with the most up-to-date items in search of things that really meet their needs. Clients of interior designers want items that are unique, for them alone. Design services cost money, and design clients like to feel that they are the only people smart enough to have found the right source and the special place to purchase from. It's their store, their designer, an important part of their lives, and part of what makes them unique individuals.

There will be more specialty shops dedicated to particular styles or needs: Victorian, Mission, Art Deco; bathroom, kitchen, or bedroom; apartment living; mature living. The style trends of the 1990s are multi-culturalism and contemporary versions of the styles of the 1930s through 1950s, with the colors of the 1960s. Clients will pre-segregate themselves by their choices.

People who buy furnishings and design services want both stability and change. They are looking for a store or a resource that seems secure and reliable; they want a reasonably good selection and the assurance what they see is the best in the industry. They also want a very good guarantee that the manufacturer or someone stands behind that furniture should anything go wrong.

They are very value oriented. They expect to get a very special price and a good deal or they're not going to use an interior designer. Today customers know that quality is possible, and not just at the highest price level. Design clients know that technology has pushed down the cost of furnishings.

Buying furniture is an emotional as well as a financial investment. Interior designers must continue to recognize and work with the emotional aspects of interior design. You may not consider working with emotions scientific, but if that is what the client wants, you will profit by addressing that need.

Industry studies of consumer furniture buyers of the past three years tell us that the clients are not shopping in as many stores as they had in the past. Our clients work hard and would rather spend time working or with their families than shopping. This is why shopping needs to be entertaining and pleasurable. People are so stressed out and busy in the rest of their lives; interior design should not be another stress.

Consumers expect designers and sales people to be able to answer questions, even those they did not know enough to ask. People don't want an uninformed body to point out that the furniture is attractive. They can see that for themselves. They want to know why the piece is great and why it should be part of their lives. They are asking for technical information and most have the background to understand it.

Clients are very impatient. They want what they want and they want it now. They want products to do exactly what they expect them to do and to be fun. They are not going to put up with things that don't meet their standards of quality or aren't exactly what they want.

Today people who want to buy furniture look for designers and stores that offer them service as well as value, and value comes at every price point. Buying new furniture is an event, and should have all the ceremony events deserve. Clients expect amenities such as a cup of coffee and a place where their children can play or be entertained while they are making their purchases.

FORGING THE LINK

Today, people are looking for someone they can trust, whose philosophy blends with theirs. The reasoning runs along these lines: "Is this the kind of person that I want to entrust my future to? I believe that my future is directed by the environment I live in. I want to be sure that the person who will be coaching me and helping me develop this is someone I can respect."

This attitude is why the client must be considered part of the design team. In almost every professional relationship today, people don't want someone who tells them what to do but a coach who considers and makes suggestions.

Recent studies indicate that one pleasurable experience will offset the stress of three negative experiences. If our mission is to improve the way people live, then turning working with an interior designer into a pleasure is a step in the right direction.

This means we have to work harder at preparing clients for the effects of change. Even though clients want what is new and different, change comes hard and every change that we've gone through has been difficult. People like things the way they used to be; it's comfortable. But that's not the way the world is run and that's not what makes our field.

So many times as designers we've been forced into taking on a new line. It was a case of having to stay up all night to learn that new program and price list, but after getting into it and mastering it, we tell people, "Oh it's easy, no problem."

The truth of it is that it is not easy! We really put effort into learning, and you learn by doing some very difficult things. So we should not say to our clients, "You're going to love that transition." We have to tell the truth. Part of getting used to new furnishings is rough, but it is a challenge, it's exciting, and it's an opportunity to live better.

Consumers come to us because they don't want IKEA or Workbench or Sears. They want things designed strictly for them—they want items in their style and size, and to their particular specifications. They know that furnishings come in sizes and that we can customize even products from other parts of the world. They want what they asked for, not a loose interpretation of it. Just as much as they want quality, they want exactly what they ordered.

Finally, consumers want what they want fast! They want things to happen today, not next week or a year from now. Because we are able to bring things to our clients much more quickly than ever before, design clients expect this fast turnaround. People are no longer *willing* to wait.

As our clients get older, they know more and have more specific demands. We have a more discriminating, better educated, and harder-to-please client base. Doing business requires more effort and a different type of presentation. We no longer have impulse buyers. The high volume easy money is gone.

We are moving from a time when getting the best price was paramount into a period in which people want quality and are willing to pay for it. Quality is a very personal judgment. Quality to an interior designer is not necessarily quality to a client. Not only do we have to know every attribute that makes a product work, we have to match it to the specific needs of the client and the locale. Clients want products that work for them, as opposed to one size fits all. Fortunately, technology has made customization less expensive.

USER-FRIENDLY DESIGN STUDIOS

Studios and furniture stores need to become more user friendly and more comfortable. The entire experience must be fresh, educational, and fun. We have to use the communication techniques people have grown accustomed to and expect. Stores and studios will have to be places where people feel comfortable.

Clients have been over-marketed. Everyone is trying to win a project. Companies that built their businesses by making cold calls no longer find cold calls effective; everyone is calling. Design marketers recommend that we pursue clients, not projects, and create cradle-to-grave relationships.

Convenience is essential. For designers, working 9 to 5 is going to be a memory. In the 90s designers, sales people, and stores work when clients have time to see us.

There are fewer large furniture stores, so design studios will have to be larger. I see a return to design studios with some inventory so that clients can test furniture for comfort and ease of use. My clients don't seem to be looking for style as much as for comfort today. Our studios will also need space for staging events.

There is power in association today. Independent designers and small companies will have ties to larger companies, or to a network of small companies. Smaller firms may, in effect, become partners with manufacturers to present new products. This will come about because our clients want to know where things come from and that an organization stands behind the merchandise.

This association works two ways. Designers are in direct contact with the consumer and can pass this information on to the manufacturers. Constant consumer feedback can be analyzed to give design directions. Manufacturers assist the retail or design firm with the in-depth customer service needed to keep clients happy for life.

We are sure to judge a woman in whose house we find ourselves for the first time, by her surroundings. We judge her temperament, her habits, her inclinations, by the interior of her home. We may talk of the weather, but we are looking at furniture.

ELSIE DE WOLFE, *The House in Good Taste*, Century Books, 1913

AREAS OF INFLUENCE

When a designer and a client come together, both should understand that they bring to the project their own experience, requirements, restrictions, and emotions. Clients are influenced by many issues, not just their environments. Everything we are exposed to in life has influence, whether positive or negative. As designers, we need to get close enough to our clients to understand what these experiences mean to them and to the project.

A number of my clients have been to design school, where they developed their visual skills. They also have been exposed to a great many parts of the interior design business. Their education program may have been different from mine. Obviously, they did not spend 30 some years working in the field as you or I have. Their work and life experiences are different, and this affects the way they see and think about things.

In fact, it is exciting to see these different components come into play. A client with a design background brings different influences and experience to a project than those brought by clients from other backgrounds. But their experience is different from your own, and you must consider this, even though you might have gone to the same school.

It is hard not to be impressed, or at least influenced by the projects published by the so-called shelter magazines—*House & Garden, Architectural Digest, Southern Accents, Country Living* and others. It is a very sophisticated and styled look. People come to us saying they want a room like the one in *Architectural Digest*. Well, this is fine, but many times those homes cost many millions of dollars and the budget for one room alone may be a million dollars. Although most people realize that the owner of the home in *Architectural Digest* is a bit wealthier than they are, they don't realize the huge investments that are made in properties. It can be difficult to explain to clients that there is a wide variation in budget.

We can explain that the budget for that room was over $4 million. We can offer to take influences and elements from that room and create a room that fits the way the client lives as well as his or her budget. Discussions of this sort can build a comfort level; the disparity between budget and reality doesn't have to be a major stumbling block.

Television and films are major influences. *The Journal of Interior Design* (formerly the *Journal of Interior Design Education and*

Research) published an article on this subject in Volume 19, No. 2, 1993, by Shauna Corry and Joann Asher Thompson, Ph.D. They conclude that the influence is direct and immediate, that high-exposure viewers prefer lifestyle design and low-exposure viewers prefer traditional design. They infer that the media may also influence the design education of students, and ask who is responsible for the content of visual images. "Because designers are influenced by visual images, both consciously and subliminally, it may be prudent to teach design students to be aware of the potential influence popular film media may have."

Television and film are pervasive, and the perspective is as untrue as you get with photography cameras. Sets for television shows are designed to telegraph a message about the characters, not to make people's lives easier through environment. And of course, no living room set for a televised series is ever cluttered.

Influences can be positive or negative. Some people might see a television show and be inspired to expand the space they have. Because they've seen something better than what they have, they begin to want it. People may look at sets designed for television shows—which are kind of simple—and realize that the clutter that they live with is perhaps eroding their thinking patterns and that they need a simpler environment. Or it may just make them want to redesign.

One of my projects was critiqued by a client's seven- or eight-year-old grandson, an avid television watcher. He visited her house when the project was substantially complete but still needed a few final touches. He commented that this was a real Ewing room (from the show *Dallas*). She sort of laughed because she had never thought of the room in that light; the style was very different. He thought the Ewing rooms were great and therefore he liked her room. This was his way of complimenting her. She didn't see it that way.

The architecture in this country was influenced by the architecture of other countries. The architecture in nearby Hershey, Pennsylvania shows several origins. Mr. Milton Hershey went to Cuba and returned to build his Moorish style hotel. Many of the other buildings in Hershey show the influence of his trips to Cuba.

His wife was a Bostonian, and you can tell which buildings she influenced. A whole community evolved this way.

We are also influenced by the people we live with. Early in my marriage, my husband said he loved a wallpaper and would not consider anything else. I really didn't think it was right for the space. But I was new in the marriage. I did the walls as he wanted them because I had chosen many of the things in our house and I felt that there should be something that was his choice. What a mistake! He had no idea how a small swatch of wallpaper translated into a large mass of space. As a result, he didn't like it and I surely didn't like it. It was one of the first things I changed, as soon as possible.

It's important for interior designers to guide our clients in their choices, to recognize the things that have influenced them, and to counteract them when appropriate. One reason people hire designers is to make sure they don't put the wrong piece of fabric on a chair or the wrong wallcovering in a certain space. Clients come to us because they want to use our experience and our eyes to select the right design elements and use them in the appropriate places.

Attitudes and opinions change over time. Anthony Torres, a designer newspaper editors loved to quote (and he used his influence well), said that it's a good idea to let children have whatever color room they want. It's very inexpensive to paint a child's room. If the child decides to live in a red room, let him or her have that experience. When they grow up they will have a much more mature attitude toward colors. He also said that if you really feel the color is awful, make it the accent color for the room, use it in a pillow, a bedspread, or a lamp, so the child sees that his opinions count. It's important to use as many of the child's choices as possible.

Everything influences us in one way or another. Some people are influenced a great deal by an article in the newspaper and other people might read it and forget it; it means nothing to them. I may save an article because one line in it made me think. That story alerted me to a forgotten issue or something that I was unaware of. And the way that I've used the one line was entirely different from what the article meant. This is the way influence works.

We gain experience through travel, through study, and through observation. People in general tend to like the styles of furnishings of people whom they like, and to have an aversion to the styles of people they don't like. All of this influences the interior spaces that we and our clients want to live with.

7

REALITY CHECK
Design Firms

The interior design profession has existed for nearly a hundred years without a formal working structure or a working theory, which is confusing to say the least. Designers work in so many different ways, unlike some more formalized professions such as medicine, law, or architecture. The one thing we have in common is an independent spirit.

PATTERNS OF SUCCESS

Today, a successful designer is the person who has the newest things first, not the person who does the traditional things very well. The old crafts are essential, especially when combined with new technology to become state of the art. It is important for a designer to have opportunities to learn and to be exposed to new technology, as well as having an extensive background in the art and science of interior design and the many crafts allied with our field.

Performance and self-reliance are the new standards.

THE INFORMATION GAP

There is a gap between interior design practice, education, and industry. Allison Carll White and Ann Whiteside Dixon at the

University of Kentucky documented it in 1992. Practitioners don't use the knowledge developed in college and university interior design programs and don't understand the value of graduate education in interior design.

The reason we don't use the knowledge developed in design education programs is that it isn't easily accessible. A strong design practice is based on knowledge. The rate of change in the world today is phenomenal. You used to be able to count on adding to your knowledge. Now we replace wholesale segments because what we knew isn't just obsolete, it has been proven wrong. I've always encouraged designers to keep learning. Knowledge and education can prepare us to deal with changes, can even equip us to be leaders in the field.

A Joel Polsky/Fixtures Furniture Forum, Vision 2010, which took place in May 1994 at the University of Kentucky in Lexington, brought together participants from design practice, education and the industry to discuss the establishment of a research agenda that supports the value of interior design. The forum said, "The value of a well-designed environment is verifiable, making interior design a critical component of the designed environment . . . the profession is supported by an expanding body of knowledge that encompasses business, art and science." The conference was one effort in bridging the gaps within the design industry.

THE WAY WE WORK

One of the reasons large design firms or large companies were formed is transaction costs. The overhead for many standard business processes was heavy enough to make it effective to share office space and the costs of office procedures, bookkeeping, and general communication.

Today, almost any repetitive business service a design firm needs can be bought; there is no need to do it in-house. There are firms that handle payroll services [ADP (Automatic Data Processing) and Paychex are two], accounting, bookkeeping, specification, billing, word processing, and financial services. Technology has simplified communication.

Technology has eroded the need and desire for the giant design firm. Often working in very small teams or groups linked to a larger resource is superior. This link can give access to credit information, business procedures, and anything else not requiring the creative aspect of design. Communications technology gives us the means to make the link and still remain individual companies.

Social structures have changed the way we work. Designers are no longer considered authority figures who could prescribe a design. Today clients are knowledgeable about design, and they ask many, many questions.

For most of us, the days of the open-ended budget are gone or limited, simply because there are fewer people with money. There are astronomically wealthy people, there are people who live well, and there are an increasing number for whom buying interior design services means sacrificing things they once considered necessities. And interior design should be considered a necessity.

Computers are no longer optional equipment for design studios. Clients can go to kitchen design centers and, in an hour or less, see on the computer how their kitchen would look in different colors and style of cabinetry. Can we match that? It is still possible to work without a CAD, but the time will come that working on a CAD will be as universal as using a telephone. And those of us who have resisted learning to use the complex CAD programs of the 1980s simply because they were so difficult can breathe more easily; CAD programs are getting simpler and more user-friendly all the time.

Although we probably won't have a lot of clients who can afford entirely custom furnishings, almost every client wants or would appreciate a piece or two that can't be bought in any department store.

One positive change is that there is a wide range of furniture and furnishings available for quick delivery. Manufacturers are ready to accommodate our special orders, and larger manufacturers are learning to act like the smaller ones. The competition is no longer large manufacturer versus large manufacturer and small versus small, but manufacturers of all sizes against each other. Technology permits the small or single-person firm to compete directly with large firms.

The focus has swung back from business-related design to home-related design, and homes must accommodate different activities. It's hard to believe that the home office would be important to the design industry, but it is. Today's cottage industries are everyone from market strategists to typists, so we know we'll be doing more home offices.

Space is valuable. The available space must be tailored to the needs and activities of the people who live in the space. Interior designers have always been asked to solve problems. We are being asked to design spaces that actively make life better, and the clients are more sophisticated. One thing we can offer is a livability assessment of the spaces, views, storage, and multiple functions a home is expected to harbor.

Our industry is in turmoil, but at least one interior design firm, Gensler & Associates Architects, is growing. The firm heads *Interior Design* magazine's list of biggest firms with annual billings of $80 million in 1993, when total revenues for the 200 biggest interior design firms dropped by 10 percent to $600 million. Gensler & Associates added 85 employees that year in an industry where employment fell by 19 percent, or 5,500 people.

The firm has grown by preparing clients for a future of telecommuting, teleconferencing, shared office space and smaller headquarters. Founder M. Arthur Gensler Jr. is known for his management skills and salesmanship. A voracious reader, his research and trend-spotting skills are admired by professional trend-spotters. This knowledge benefits clients as well as the firm. The firm also relies heavily on communications networks and computers to maintain common standards and identity thoughout its 14 offices in the United States and Pacific Rim countries, so client know precisely what they are getting when they go to Gensler.

MYSTIQUE VERSUS VALUE

If no one understands what we do, we must be doing something wrong. No one outside the industry knows what an interior designer does. Is it mystique or lack of awareness? Right now there are 74 hundred different definitions for interior designer, depending on who you ask. Even people who have worked with interior designers can't say what we do.

The two main functions of interior design are to educate and distribute. In the narrowest interpretation, we educate our clients so they can make appropriate choices, and we distribute products, installing them in homes and work places.

Obviously this is too focused a definition. Interior design has an impact on the quality of life. We also have to educate our clients about what we have done and how it affects their lives. We need to define interior design constantly, to educate people through our actions. More importantly, we need to put our information in the language of that specific consumer—the store owner, corporation, or empty-nester.

Business people are typically uneasy with designers. "Business people tend to see design as a matter of styling; something you do to a product after the important work—the engineering—is done," says Paul Brayton, CEO of Brayton International. "It is time for designers and business people to work at seeing themselves as partners in a process that benefits everybody."

To Brayton, design is a competitive advantage, "the intelligent application of resources to providing for human needs." And the market, the undifferentiated mass of potential clients, is very aware that one size does not fit all and demands customization of designs for local needs. Tom Peters, author of books on business management, says "design may be the most potent tool for differentiating one's products or services."

Tom Peters also says that design should take an equal and early seat at the head table, on board at the creation of the dream and an equal partner throughout. He is entirely correct, but he had to learn this through experience, the experience of working with a designer to shape a book.

Where interior design fails is in communicating its value. We have to start educating people about the value of interior design, and we cannot do that unless we ourselves believe that interior design has value. Long ago the architectural profession narrowed its definition of architecture to exclude interior design; that doesn't make interior design any less valuable. Interior design may be a crazy amalgam of science (which has measurable effects) and art (which is abstract), but the effects of interior design are measurable.

More than one designer has suggested that educators and practicing professionals should collaborate on developing design studios, lectures, and public exhibitions to raise awareness that well-designed facilities can be enhance the quality of life.

Cheryl Duvall, 1992-1993 president of the Institute of Business Designers (IBD), suggested that interior designers should comment on environments, good and bad. When you are in a doctor's office that has a great waiting room, say so. When a store design makes you want to go in and shop, say so. If a space is attractive and accommodates the handicapped, compliment the owner on the grace and awareness of the solution.

Certain issues are inescapable, but their tie-in to interior design may not be obvious to the consumer. You can't go a week without seeing television or reading newspaper stories on repetitive stress injuries, indoor air quality, worker productivity, and the Americans With Disabilities Act. Talk with your friends and your family about how your work addresses these issues.

If interior design is a service industry, then the designer-client relationship is the key to continuing to do business. The key to the designer-client relationship is communication.

Marilyn Farrow, 1994-1995 president of IBD, says designers should measure the differences made in the client's productivity based on the newly designed work environment and provide statistics from the client's perspective, not the design perspective. When we give corporate clients examples, success stories, they should be in the language of the boardroom.

"What isn't being offered to the client is the type of information developed through case studies. The client isn't aware of how we improved productivity, reduced absenteeism, and lowered employee turnover by creating a safe, productive, healthy and accessible environment unless we tell them," Farrow said.

I believe that design awareness has to be taught, and it should be taught in kindergarten and elementary schools as part of the basic curricula. In social studies, discuss how Frank Lloyd Wright tried to change the way secretaries sat by designing three-legged chairs for the secretarial pool at Johnson Wax. In history, talk about why the Senate chambers have very high ceilings and how this affects the way senators behave toward each other. When the effects of light are discussed in science class, mention that choosing specific lighting for specific functions is one of the things interior designers do. Harvard Business School teaches case histories that involve industrial design. We need to take our interior design experience into schools at all levels.

Interior design needs to be defined in terms of market expectations, what the market wants and expects from us. We're not doing that yet. We have the information. All we have to is pull it together and make it accessible, and then we've got it made.

INTERIOR DESIGN IS AN ART AND A SCIENCE

God is in the details.   Ludwig Mies van der Rohe

Interior design may have started as the child of decorative arts and architecture, but that was over a hundred years ago, and many sciences have contributed to the body of knowledge.

Are we designers or artists? Roger Yee, editor of *Contract Design* magazine, asks in a 1993 editorial, "Are designers trained to see themselves as artists conversant with technology whereas society wants them to perform more like technicians who are facile with art?" It's not that simple, Roger.

Interior design is a service industry, and practicing interior designers are trained observers, just like doctors, sociologists, and other scientists. Behavioral psychologists make recommendations based on their observations; so do interior designers. Art creates a mood; so do theatrical set design and interior design.

Knowledge and education are crucial elements of being a designer. In a hundred years, the field has both narrowed and broadened. Designers need more in-depth technical knowledge today, so it is no longer possible to be a generalist. At the same time, our understanding of the work is deeper and wider. Interior design was never just about selecting pretty fabrics. It's about using space to support a range of human activities and the behavioral effects of those colors, textures, and spatial arrangements on the people who live in the space.

Interior design is rooted in the practical. Elsie de Wolfe may have been "the Chintz Lady," but suitability, simplicity, and proportion were as important to her as beauty, comfort, and peace of mind.

People tend to forget that. It is true that Edith Wharton (with architect Ogden Codman) wrote the first book on interior design to alleviate the boredom and frustration of her marriage, that Elsie de Wolfe was almost 40 when she first sought design clients, that after World War I it became fashionable in England for women to have careers as interior designers, and that interior design was in part a way for the middle class to buy into an aristocratic way of life.

It is true, but to characterize interior design as the profession of bored housewives catering to the nouveaux-riches and wannabes lies by omission. Practicality and democracy have always been as important as beauty.

Interior design affects the way people behave. This is central to the practice of interior design. Interior design is a humanist science that draws on research from many other sciences. The most useful research is observation of the way people respond to things. Interior design requires knowledge that is sometimes technical and sometimes artistic.

Interior designers have been described as operating at a pre-empirical intuitive level, but we don't have to design by hunch and guesswork today. Much of our so-called intuitive knowledge has been documented by a discipline known as human factors. In the 25 years since psychologist Robert Sommer wrote that opinion, the specialty of human factors has amassed a body of research with contributions from a variety of sciences. Many of the insights in the area of human factors research come from the sociology and psychology fields.

The designer is not a mystic, a dictator, or a god. I believe interior designers should operate in the same manner as the physician who is your team member in helping with your medical problem. You don't walk into a doctor's office and accept everything that he says as absolute, as we might have done in the 1950s and 1960s. But you respect the doctor's experience, and the doctor bears the responsibility for bringing you the right type of medicine. As designers, we are responsible for bringing the right type of design to the public.

Your client group is people who share a standard of living, celebrate similar events, and admire similar qualities and ways of doing things. That combines anthropology and sociology. The study of interior design draws on anthropomorphic measurements, acoustics, illumination, olfaction, kinesics, ergonomics, color psychology, cultural bias, and sociology. Let's not forget building codes and regulations.

Interior design is a science. Science is inexact and changeable. Every day, research is published that applies to the practice of interior design. Sometimes it is proprietary research from manufacturers, or an industry White Paper. Sometimes essential information can be found in the research papers of design students. Sometimes it is in newspaper reports of business trends.

Since this information is available to us, it would seem appropriate that we incorporate it into all our design projects. Because we are designers and our work helps create the environment, we are, in effect, leaders of human behavior. The information is available, but some is hard to get. And as a consequence, some designers unknowingly create environments that encourage the wrong behaviors. It is our responsibility to create the best environments we possibly can.

FINANCE

Interior design, architectural, and engineering firms have always been seriously undercapitalized. This means it has been easy to enter the business but often very difficult to succeed. Running a business from home, starting small, and planning carefully to position yourself financially and professionally is common in the interior design industry. A design business also allows people to nurture their skills and talents and cultivate the business into a job that pays well. This category of business often appeals to women.

Businesses started by women may have the edge in times of no credit, according to a February 21, 1992 article in the *Wall Street Journal*. Three out of four women entrepreneurs started with their own financing. They couldn't get credit in the 80s, but in the 90s when banks began calling in loans, this didn't affect them because they had no loans to call in. A past director of the Small Business Administration offers another reason businesses run by women may have an edge during a recession. "Women are not the risk-takers that men are," says Alice Brown. "They are more likely to start smaller than men, with less debt, less overhead, less everything."

In the near future, interior design firms are going to need more capital to start up and more capital to keep running. We need certain pieces of equipment, and we need capital during the projects. This is not often easy to secure without prime financing.

The days of interior design businesses being poorly managed from a financial aspect are definitely over. There is a much greater need for careful management of each account; there is also a greater respect for good financial management. If you don't have the money to run the business properly, then you must consider other ways of working.

Even well-run efficient firms need changes in the current system. The answer may be some form of merger, to share the capital among us rather than having it assumed by a single organization. Can we share overhead by moving to shared spaces? We have to find ways to get top level services and equipment at lower cost.

Credit

One of the sore points in this industry is that credit is available to everyone else, but when designers ask for credit with manufacturers, there is very little credit available. Historically, many interior design firms and even some industry jobbers went into business without enough capital, and used the client's furniture deposit to run their company. Economically healthy resource firms avoided the cost of checking credit for one-time customers, preferring to deal with repeat customers, the design firms.

Today, most clients are expected to pay a deposit and a pro forma, which means they pay for the merchandise before it is delivered. Most clients do not want to pay for expensive custom merchandise until they have had a chance to see that it was done the way they asked and that it's in good condition. The 1990s is a time of customer service. The deposit and pro forma practice is going out of style.

Design firms have to decide whether they want the risks of managing the account, of paying credit and being responsible for it, or whether they would rather accept fees and let the clients be responsible for paying for furniture and furnishings.

More and more individual vendors are contracting for the design and the total product used—especially in medium sized jobs—being responsible for it, and handling the paper or the credit. This gives the client a completed project and a standard payment process.

The decision of how to handle credit may not be one designers can make. Many new suppliers of quality merchandise sell indiscriminately to designers and consumers. A national credit rating system is one suggested solution; credit insurance is another.

Credit and a good financial structure must be easily available and clearly defined for our profession to evolve.

Compensation

Compensation will in the very near future be performance-based. Many jobs have been based on salary and the path up the hierarchical ladder. Today it is a question of what you can do, not how many years you have been doing it.

In many cases, interior designers will not be on salary to a single firm, but will consult and work with many design firms throughout the country. This is the trend in other industries and there is no reason to think it will not spread to ours.

This means that we must develop new compensation plans, especially in the areas of entitlements (insurances, retirement plans, and so on). Ideally, medical insurance and retirement benefits will not be tied to the company but to the individual. Professional associations could be very helpful in offering investment, insurance, and retirement programs, to give our field the benefits that had previously been available through large corporations.

Accounting

Design firms will be handling a larger volume of business much more quickly. I believe it is possible to handle both large and small accounts.

The cost of managing projects may change who we accept and keep as clients. One reason design firms continue to lose capital is that we really do too much for the money we are paid. Not every project requires the same intensity of effort and involvement, and design firms need work at a variety of levels. We need to determine what level of work the client wants and expects, and then deliver it so that it is still profitable.

Staying in business isn't just getting accounts; it also involves looking at which accounts are price effective. After determining what types of accounts were practical and profitable, one design firm found that some were too expensive to handle. The firm suggested to these clients that they either enlarge the account or that they use another firm. The firm lost $120,000 worth of business, but it had cost $150,000 a year to manage those accounts. By eliminating those accounts, they had a profit of $30,000.

Designers' attitudes about money hold them back, Mary Ann Bryan, ASID, hypothesizes (*Interiors & Sources,* June 1994). She believes that the money mindset of designers makes them feel uncomfortable talking directly about money even though they are quite often successful and efficient in handling their clients' money and budgets.

Bryan assumes the problem mindset comes from a sneaking disbelief that what designers do is worth paying for. Money is a measure of success. The effects of design are an abstract. The problem lies in translating this abstract into a dollar value. But designers are trained to solve problems and create order from chaos. We should be able to believe ourselves when we say that a chaotic environment is destructive, and that an environment that works well increases productivity and satisfaction.

Profit Ratio

What should the profit ratio be? This varies depending on the firm's structure. Some firms, whose profits had been as high as 15 to 16 percent of net profit before taxes, now find it is only consider 10 and 12 percent. Clients come to us with set budgets and time schedules, and if one design firm isn't willing to do the job, the next one will.

Please don't think I am saying that investing in the stock market is a better way to earn a living. Interior design or a related business can bring in a better return on investment than a typical stock market investment. And there are creative dividends in the energy we get from the constant change and challenges.

Will design fees ever grow again? It has always been possible to charge a higher fee for a unique product or service. The perception of value provides the edge.

8

A MISSION FOR
THE INTERIOR DESIGN FIELD

"I have always found," said Mr. Pullman, "that people are great-
ly influenced by their physical surroundings. Take the roughest man, a
man whose lines have brought him into the coarsest and poorest sur-
roundings, and bring him into a room elegantly carpeted and finished,
and the effect on his bearing is immediate. The more artistic and refined
the external surroundings, the better and more refined the man."
RUSSELL LYNES, *The Tastemakers* (Westport, Connecticut,
Greenwood Press, 1983, page 95)

Good interior design is responsible design. It takes into account
the needs and realities of the situation and of the people who will
use the space. This approach to interior design looks to the future
rather than waiting for a problem to occur. It goes beyond pretti-
fying a room or responding to environmental issues raised by the
media. If we address real needs with well-researched solutions,
then interior design will be indispensable.

DESIGN AFFECTS BEHAVIOR

Environments direct human behavior, and, because of it, interior
designers have a responsibility to the future culture to design
spaces dedicated to the needs of people of varying ages and physical abilities, and to permitting all types of activities—private,
work-related, or community.

The concept that interior design can change the way people live and think is older than the field of interior design. The Willow Tea-Room designed by Charles Rennie Mackintosh was a project to fight drunkenness in Glasgow at the turn of the century. In the 1930s Sherrill Whiton described a goal of interior design as "to produce a unified composition and a desired aesthetic and psychological effect." "Virtually everything that man is and does is associated with the experience of space." Anthropologist Edward T. Hall wrote that in 1966, and in 1969 psychologist Robert Sommer wrote that "designers are shaping people as well as buildings."

Interior design educator John Pile wrote in 1988 that "Human beings are powerfully affected by their particular environment and the related connection that human behavior is in turn affected by the environment in which it occurs."

That environment affects behavior is proved by every project we do. In over 25 years of working with the Milton Hershey School in Hershey, Pennsylvania, I have seen interior design help change lives. Children from deprived, neglected, and destructive backgrounds who came to the school later left this nurturing environment as accomplishing professionals with professional and personal skills. In the pleasant and attractive Milton Hershey School environment, they are given a new way to live and the physical trappings—usually clothing—to reinforce the new life.

A great many of them changed just because of the exposure to a controlled environment with furnishings that were geared toward their development. We made sure that everything from the chair they sat on to the view they saw was designed to enrich their educational and social development. The direction of this experiment in behavior was determined by noted psychotherapists, sociologists, and educators, and with the input of the students aged five on up. And the changes are dramatic.

Another example of environment that changes behavior is in Founder's Hall at Hershey. People might be boisterous and loud outside, but once they came through the doors there was perfect silence, because it is an awe-inspiring, dramatic building. It sets a tone of respect for the space, the institution, and the overall objectives of that institution. Part of the effect is due to the high ceilings and the sheer size of the interior space, a technique architects and designers employ in other community buildings designed as areas of respect, celebration, and cultural enrichment.

Church design has changed since the 1960s to accommodate a more participatory style of services, where the congregation and the ministers interact. (The Catholic Church is an extreme example of this.) Therefore some of the church design, which worked well for an older philosophy and liturgical style, does not work for the new liturgy. We have moved from a mystical, hierarchical style of worship to a more egalitarian one, and church spaces are much more intimate than they were.

DESIGNERS AS AGENTS OF CHANGE

Business is the engine of modern society and will play a dominant role in shaping the future. This makes people in business responsible for the quality of our future, according to Rinaldos Brutoco, founder of the World Business Academy. Thus, people in business must act as trustees for human society.

Many countries have stronger links through business than through politics. When business and medical centers talked to each other, they got along fine. The political leaders were still arguing, but the businesses got along because there is a certain basic understanding within a discipline. Coming together for business purposes gave people from many countries experience with different ways of life, and this helped shape their new directions. Contact is important. It changes faceless countries into countries full of people, and people make changes.

Today's new direction is not going to be a result of action by government or religion, but because of individual businesses.

I take this one step further. I believe that interior design shapes human behavior. Communication is even affected by the placement of chairs; this can influence the way people react to each other. Because interior design shapes human behavior, and because people in business shape the world, I think the field of interior design should acknowledge this and take some responsibility. We are the engineers, we are the leaders, we are the designers of tomorrow.

Rather than just responding to the requests of our clients, we need to demonstrate that interior design is a powerful element in the process of change.

The future of our field is in identifying a mission and linking together resources and designers to achieve this goal. Interior design can show people how to deal more effectively with each other through the effective design of space. We could almost make a religion of it. The interior design field could be the Mother Theresa of environment.

There is a story about a highly successful American business woman who felt her life was not fulfilling. She wrote to Mother Theresa and asked if she could join her mission in Calcutta. Months went by. Finally, Mother Theresa responded with a letter one sentence long: Thank you very much for your interest, but find your own Calcutta.

Interior design has its own Calcutta right here. Changing behavior by changing the quality of the environment is broad enough in scope to keep us all busy, and challenging enough to be worth our interest and creativity.

From my experience with the Milton Hershey School and every other project in my career, I have come to the conclusion that designers *are responsible* for directing behavior. We need to take this responsibility seriously.

ENVIRONMENT MAKES A DIFFERENCE

Doesn't cultural deprivation lead to spiritual destruction? Today acute problems in human behavior include crime on the streets, teenage drugs and violence, and more. When you think of the homes that these teenagers are coming from, and the schools in which they are being educated, you see that not much is being done to develop their self-esteem. And since we know that environment can make a difference, it seems that upgrading the environment would be an effective and inexpensive method of changing the world.

It seems to me that some of these issues should be dealt with in design schools as a standard part of our training. Perhaps our professional associations should target an issue and challenge us to invent solutions.

A local housing project wanted me to design and furnish one of their standard homes with a budget of $2,000. I thought it was a great opportunity for students, and was able to involve a class of design students at the Bradley School. Together, we established budgets for each room, evaluated likely storage needs, and set a schedule. After coming up with viable floor plans, the students shopped at the local Goodwill Store and low-cost department stores. They did simple painting and installations themselves. The home looked terrific and worked well, and the students gained practical experience.

A socially responsible design education is integral to the health and prosperity of the design and architectural professions and the people who use their products and services, according to Professor Leslie Kane Weisman, an associate professor of architecture at the New Jersey Institute of Technology. Students in her course "Architecture and Social Change" are required to volunteer 20 hours of community service to a nonprofit agency addressing social problems dealt with in the course.

"When students realize they are responsible and accountable to others as designers, they begin to design in an empathic mode, allowing them to empower others through their work rather than merely imposing their own images upon the world," Professor Weisman says.

The American Society of Interior Designers (ASID) has given awards to a number of groups within chapters that have undertaken design projects for charity. But attention to practical human needs should be the focus of our business, not something we use only for charity projects!

Many design projects deal directly with current issues: renovating housing projects for the economically deprived, making existing buildings more accessible in compliance with the Americans with Disabilities Act, and creating interiors that use less energy or are more ergonomically correct. And social problems can be eased through interior design. I don't think anyone in our field deals with every single problem completely.

Professor Weisman spent ten years putting together a book that discusses man-made space and how those spaces limit human beings and exclude, dismiss, and devalue women, minorities, and other marginalized groups. *Discrimination by Design: A Feminist Critique of the Man-Made Environment* (University of Illinois Press, 1992) targets a whole realm of spaces in which designers and architects can rewrite public opinion of the design industry.

USE DESIGN TO BUILD A SENSE OF COMMUNITY

In its most basic form, a community is a group of people who have made a commitment to communicate with each other at an increasingly meaningful level. At a more sophisticated level, a community is a group that can speak together with a unified voice.

Dr. M. Scott Peck, *The Different Drum*

Some current design work is remarkable. Health centers and indoor tennis clubs stimulate physical activity and remove some of the limits of climate. What other activities could also be expanded through the use of interior space? But we might perhaps build communities around some of these activities instead of building them around shopping centers, which seems to be the trend right now.

So let's not talk about designing only luxury spaces, or for businesses, which are somewhat organized to begin with. What about spaces that need organizational structure or direction, such as spaces that build community?

The old cities and towns compelled interaction. If you walked past a shoemaker's shop, you said hello. You could observe behavior of many socioeconomic levels. It was possible for a needy child to emulate a doctor or a lawyer, the way they walked, talked and interacted with people. You came into frequent contact with role models.

Today we are living in our own ghettoes with our own barriers. It doesn't matter whether you are a factory worker, a moderately well-paid professional, or a very wealthy executive. Our lifestyles are boundaries and we don't often have contact with people whose lifestyles aren't pretty much the same as our own. I believe interior design can change that—not 100 percent, and not alone, but design is part of the solution. **When we build walls, we create wars. If we are going to live together, we need areas that build community.**

In the 1990s, major bookstores are positioning themselves as hangouts or clubs. I saw a nanny with two preschool children napping in a stroller as she sat and read. A retired gentleman sat at a table drinking coffee and comparing several books from a large pile. A group of college students discussed something in great detail at another table. This is wonderful.

Our work affects behavior whether we intend it or not. Let's consider how to create spaces that direct behavior appropriately.

RESPONSIBILITY TO KEEP LEARNING

I think interior designers who have not refreshed their learning are just as lax and potentially dangerous as doctors who left medical school in 1965 and haven't cracked a book or attended a seminar since. It's morally wrong, because the term interior designer carries an implied background and knowledge. When you practice with incomplete or inadequate knowledge, you are not only cheating yourself and your clients of a good project, but you may also be creating a dangerous environment.

A designer who sees that the client has a low-vision problem or some physical impairment and does not tactfully offer design options that will improve that person's quality of life is just as behind the times and just as dangerous to society as a medical doctor who realizes his client has high blood pressure and doesn't suggest changes that will help control the problem.

It is a matter of attitude. If you knew that tomorrow you were going to perform leading-edge work that meant life or death to someone, you would brush up on your techniques, call people who had done that procedure, and review a video of the procedure. If you expected to be doing the same thing tomorrow that you have done for 62 years and it is no more engrossing that sweeping a floor, what's the point of refining your techniques?

I see designer and leader as synonymous. If you are a leader, you have a responsibility. You have a responsibility to the person who can't keep up with the group, whether that person has low vision, mobility problems, or some other idiosyncrasy. Even if the people you are leading are more capable, your responsibility is to develop them within the range of their capabilities.

Interior designers are educators as well as leaders. As educators, we must realize that if we are going to improve the way society lives, designers must play a major role. We can't blame society's problems on the police force, the government, and other people! We have to examine our roles. If design is an influential element— as I think it is, and as human factors research supports—then individual designers have perhaps more power to change things than any other profession.

Doing nothing is amoral. It is sinful, in a sense, because we have knowledge; we know that we can improve environments and in doing so improve the quality of people's lives. Changing behavior through interior design is peaceful. We don't look like we're doing anything wrong. In doing our jobs, we cause no deliberate harm. We're not going out and shooting people. But we may be doing worse things without realizing it. In designing an environment inappropriately, how many lives are we destroying?

Design is a cultural development tool, and we must use it as a tool. Interior designers should not wait to respond as victims. We should want to direct or design as leaders.

Through designing educational facilities, I learned that different age groups respond differently to different environments. Younger children need much more stimulation through color to keep them excited and to give a fun feeling to a space, while older students may need a quieter space for more long term learning. The acoustical aspects of the space, how well we hear, how our vision is directed, and all of our senses need to be dealt with when designing spaces.

Walt Disney was a pioneer in creating physical demonstrations of this. In Disney World and at Epcot Center, it is not only what we see, but what we touch, hear, and even smell. As a result, the experience is beyond the visual—it is all encompassing and therefore our receivers operate at a higher capacity.

CONSIDER HUMAN NEEDS

Let's pose the question: What should interior design be doing that it is not doing today? What designers should be doing today is design that improves social dynamics for all people, not just the wealthy and the middle class.

What I care about is how a particular person feels in a given situation, not the age of the building. Is it possible to put five-year-old children in spaces that are really great for five-year-olds? Can we provide the right environment for students studying calculus, one that enhances their ability to acquire knowledge? Are we giving people who are ill an environment that supports them, one that goes beyond simply not harming them but also provides the diversity necessary for comfort and allows them to feel they have some control over the environment? Have we given them the ability to control even the lighting or acoustics?

We have to return to looking first at human needs, not what we can do with the building.

This is not to say I cannot appreciate artistic buildings. We need some monuments to our society. But a building dedicated to a specific function should work. The Frank Lloyd Wright Group did a facility in Ohio for Alzheimers' patients. Typically Alzheimers' patients have memory retention problems, and fear and rage are a common result. The group investigated the kinds and sizes of spaces that Alzheimers' patients are comfortable with. Rather than using colors and numbers to help identify rooms, the Wright Group placed a showcase at the entrance of each room to house the patient's own memorabilia. This made it easier for patients to identify their rooms, and decreased the likelihood of confusion and paralyzing fear.

This is the way interior designers need to look at every person and every activity. We need the same emphasis and study of everyday activities, such as the way a mother holds her baby or the way people move on the street, as has been devoted to studying the cockpits of airplanes to determine what holds the attention and what is ergonomically comfortable for a pilot. There are a lot more mothers and babies than there are pilots.

The winter of 1993-1994 dumped enormous amounts of ice and snow on the Northeast. If this is the weather wave of the future, we need to change our streets to decrease the numbers of people falling and breaking legs and arms on the snow and ice. If our climate is changing, design elements can make the environment less hazardous.

The ramps incorporated into many buildings for wheelchair access are too often obstacles; other people fall over them! This is something human factors specialists, ethologists, anthropologists, ergonomists, and the other sciences should investigate and change.

Cynthia Leibrock, founder of Easy Access Barrier Free Design, agrees. "Designers' knowledge of aesthetics allows them to integrate technology into the environment. No one with a physical difference wants to be stigmatized by that difference. I've seen elderly people struggle up stairs rather than use a ramp or a lift because it draws so much attention to them. Until technology is integrated in a way that is visually pleasing, it's seldom used."

Malls, as community spaces, should be studied. In a mall, you're not paying attention to where you put your feet; you are looking at store windows, carts, people, and live displays. Multiple levels and short flights of stairs are common to malls, and are hazardous. It's downright scary because you find yourself looking in the shop window, which is what you're supposed to be doing in a mall, and not seeing a stair step. To me, that is bad design.

I have to wonder about design priorities. Sometimes clients are so insistent on making an impact with design that they lose the function. Sometimes showrooms are so ornate that you don't notice the product, and that's not what interior design is supposed to be doing.

HUMAN FACTORS

Human factors means fitting the client with the right products. For instance, I took a married couple into a bathroom fixtures showroom and had them try different toilets. They tested the contours of the American seat versus the French to determine which contour was most comfortable. They tested different heights because as people grow older, the height of a toilet becomes a critical issue. For the gentleman of the house, who is tall, we chose an 18-inch toilet. For the woman, who was not as tall, we chose a 16-inch one.

The standard toilet in modern dwellings is 14 inches, and is not going to be great for these people as they age. It might be okay today, but give them another 10 years or so and they're going to find it a problem. People used to stay in a home seven to ten years. These clients have been in their present home for 25 years and are remodelling it because they like being there. I'm sure they will be there another 25 years. The time to deal with potential problems is now, when they are redesigning their home.

Considering human factors is just good business practice. The point is that when a client wants a bathroom with unusual faucets, it's fine if the client is the only one who uses it. That client will soon learn how to turn it on and off. But for public spaces or family spaces used by the visiting mother-in-law, mother, and grandfather, this may not be good because it will take them awhile to figure out which is hot and which is cold. And they could scald themselves if they turn the faucet incorrectly.

We need to look at where artistry is appropriate. If it is your own personal space and you want something very different because it makes you smile every time you use it — that's wonderful! You'll learn its quirks and it won't be a problem. When more than one person will use the space, I think we have to be a lot more universal in our designs.

Good design makes the best public relations. Interior design that meets the needs of today automatically promotes the entire field. Everyone who touches the space cannot help but see and feel the difference. On the other hand, if we try to promote a need or issue based on past problems, we are wasting time and money and making our field obsolete.

MISSION STATEMENTS

You hear a lot about mission statements these days. All it really amounts to is that businesses with a vision, goal, or direction of where they want to be and how they want to do it are succeeding.

A mission is a very clearly defined direction or focus. It is an accomplishable goal. There is an end point and benchmarks to reach in accomplishing that goal. By defining the objective of your practice, you establish your orientation and your focus. What is valuable to you?

The mission statement at my firm is to provide the best possible service to our clients and to enhance their lives to the greatest extent attainable through interior design. We want to keep our clients for life and we want to be part of their development.

What the home furnishings and design industry really needs is a mission statement. This is a service industry. The mission statement should focus on how the industry can best meet the needs of the customer.

A great design industry is composed of talented people and resources dedicated to using the scientific and artistic tools of design to enhance the way our clients live and work.

Designers must know the details of products in order to specify them for the right uses.

Resources must seek out information from the designer about customer needs in order to produce the right products.

When resources and designers come together to produce what the client wants and needs, clients will be better able to appreciate our value.

So many of the problems with products can be easily remedied with current technology. There is no excuse for lack of communication.

THE OFFICE ENVIRONMENT

An office is an artificial environment. It can be designed to support human activities, or it can erode their health and productivity. A highly technical body of knowledge and esthetics goes into office design these days, but in practice some of it seems less than beneficial.

There is too much at stake in work environments for design to be based simply on good taste. Designers need to use consultants who can provide them and their clients with information on human response. The neutral, unadorned spaces of the Shakers worked in part because they were residential and in part because they were small and used for a variety of tasks. In offices, over-large, stark spaces cause anxiety.

Office environments have physical, cultural, and psychological effects on all human beings. We spend many hours every day working in offices. Every component of the office environment spurs a human response. Those who design offices—whether they are professional architects, interior designers or facility managers—must have input from other disciplines.

Too many offices have been designed to suit the tastes of the planners, and not for the best use by the people who must work there. It's true that many of these planners have good taste, and that the resulting spaces may look great. It's even true that their clients may have been initially thrilled by the resulting spaces.

But the test of an office is in the way it works. Before an office design is recognized with a design award, these questions should be asked of office workers: Does the space make your job any easier? Do you feel less fatigued at the end of the week because of the time you have spent in this controlled environment?

Too often magazines show newly designed office space that competes with Shaker interiors for simplicity, a pared-down, almost barren style that uses neutral colors and nothing else. The concept has its appeal; offices should not be too stimulating. Monochrome seems executive and elegant. For employees who had been working in transitional spaces that had been minimally upgraded for their specific tasks and were overcrowded besides, large spaces in a plain basic color seemed a welcome relief.

Even the most beautiful environment can have its faults. Some of the elements that affect the ability of people to work in them are lighting; lack of individual control; indoor pollution from furniture, carpeting, and paint; lack of variety or too much variety in surface textures; the distances between workstations, both actual and perceived; color; and whether a building appears to care for its inhabitants. If the lighting was standard cool-white fluorescents, that has an effect. Studies have shown that radiation shields and full spectrum fluorescents quiet hyperactivity and improve general well-being.

Certainly, some of the office interiors shown in magazines seemed uncaring, cold, stark, neutral, and monotonous. The overuse of a single neutral color is common to many of these offices. Often the color of choice is a charcoal gray, which can be dramatic when accented with bright colors.

An executive whose firm had just moved into a new building told me an eerie story. Not a week went by without their hearing the wail of an ambulance. The company nurse said she had never seen so many instances of hypertension, high blood pressure, and depression. There had been more visits to the health suite than ever before in the history of the company. Everyone had been excited to be in this beautiful, spacious, quality environment. Why was this happening?

In the brand-new building, everything was the same intensity, and gray with no variation is boring and tedious. Color specialists say that people become nervous and edgy when in all-white, all-beige, or all-gray space; that we need contrasts for physical comfort. In fact, human beings need interiors that echo the natural spectrum as much as possible.

A dangerously monochrome environment like this can be improved but not totally fixed. Contrasts, both light and dark, must be carefully chosen and introduced. Naturally, their location affects the outcome. The designer must have an understanding not just of the item but also of its relationship to the items around it. The space can be made to seem more human by adding softer textures. Individual control could be added, but in a way that does not interfere with the operation of the building as a whole.

It is not simply the choice of color that is important, but the shades, textures, location, and the way light hits different surfaces. Today there is scientific information available on which colors are right for which items. And even basic books show how colors affect each other, and how to balance bright and cool tones.

The Lighthouse for the Blind has come up with new guidelines for effective color contrasts for people with low vision. Dark colors from the spectral extremes should be paired with high lightness colors from the mid-spectrum.

ADA Accessibility Guidelines state that the key to enhance color discrimination is to maximize luminance contrast (measured as the difference between intensities of light reflected from the foreground and background of a pattern).

Good taste is not enough. To me, design is successful and worthy of being called good design only when it answers the needs of the people who live and work in it, and is pleasant to look at as well. Today we can do so much to make environments suitable to their functions because we have better and more in-depth information.

NOISE POLLUTION

Noise can diminish your concentration and your productivity, and even harm your health, but good interior acoustical design can decrease most noise problems. Recently I was in a physician's waiting room. As I tried to read, my concentration kept being broken by everyday noise. Everything that went on at the secretary/receptionist's desk was too loud: the stapler, the shuffling of paper, the ringing of the telephone, the clatter of the typewriter. The speaker for the piped-in music was at her end of the room, and she had to speak over it as she used the phone.

At 11:45 A.M. I heard her say that she was getting a headache, and I was not surprised; so was I. The acoustic design of the room amplified all normal sounds to the level of noise. With the exception of the carpet, every surface in the room was hard. Above the desk, the ceiling was very low, causing the sound to reverberate even more. Even the lighting was annoying. Two bright downlights bounced light off her desk.

Noise is simply unwanted sound. Although we are not comfortable in complete silence, the level and type of noise we are subjected to should be controlled for optimum productivity. Sound from typewriters, computer printers, and other equipment is not only disturbing but will cause hearing impairment. It is said that a woman who vacuums her rug weekly will have impaired hearing by the time she is 40 years old, so just think what noisy equipment can do.

Soundproofing, or blocking noise from another room or area, can be done in the design of the wall system. However, care must be taken to see that the blocking is complete because anywhere air can pass, sound also comes through. The wall must extend through the ceiling to the underside of the floor above. Space around light fixtures, HVAC ducts, and other utilities may allow air and sound to leak through. To block the sound, the space must be closed. For the Enron Corporation of Houston, isolating sound was important enough to have systems furniture panels retooled to eliminate a one-quarter inch gap.

Acoustical privacy means different things to different people. When you visit the office of a professional, you expect to be seen in a private room with the door closed. The professional may know that the person in the next room can hear everything. If that same client is interviewed in an open office, a panelled landscape area where the acoustics may be technically better, he or she is usually uncomfortable. We perceive privacy as being afforded by walls and a door that closes. So privacy is a combination of physical and psychological factors.

Incidentally, the cost of space is one reason sound control has become so important. The more space there is between individual work areas, the easier it is to control sound. Fortunately much is known about sound control and there are practical ways to control the source of the noise. The closer to the source you control it, the better the sound management. For example, most noise in an office occurs near desk level, so sound absorptive materials should be used at this level.

Acoustical ceiling tiles are four or more feet above the source of the noise and are not nearly as effective at controlling sound within an area because the sound must travel before being absorbed. These tiles are highly effective at preventing the sound from disturbing the people who work above that space.

Sound is fatiguing, so when sound levels are controlled in an office, the staff will find they are less tired at the end of the day, and will come to work less tired the next day.

There is a chain reaction caused by working in acoustically appropriate space. In a well-designed space, it is not necessary to speak loudly to be understood, common sounds are not disruptive, and the whole atmosphere becomes more comfortable. People no longer need to make noise just to prove they exist. When people lose their hearing or cannot hear well, they speak more loudly to compensate. The loudest college dormitories are those for deaf students, because they can't hear how much noise they are making.

A room that has both soft (sound-absorbing) and hard surfaces (sound-reflective) placed appropriately makes communicating easier by letting us talk more softly. While I was doing a program for the Austin Corporation in Cleveland, I experienced the ultimate in acoustical design for lecture halls. Before the program began I was on stage and speaking quietly about personal things to a friend I had not seen for several months. Later I learned that everyone in the hall, even those in the back row, could hear every word we had said. That is the sign of a very well-designed lecture hall, for the speaker to be able to talk in a normal speaking voice, without a microphone, and be heard clearly by everyone.

Just as acoustical privacy means different things to different people, so does sound control. Typically, top executives are most comfortable when the sounds outside their own work spaces are reduced to an indistinguishable hum. They would prefer to hear only the noise they generate. But support staff and those for whom coming to work provides most of their social interaction want to hear what other people are doing. I heard of a building where after sound blocking and sound masking had been installed, the staff became so unbalanced due to uncontrolled sound that they destroyed the building, literally tearing vinyl wallcovering off the walls and yanking out paper towel holders in the restrooms.

Good acoustical control usually requires balancing sound absorption with sound masking, because the same materials that minimize unwanted sound also eliminate useful background sounds. Early sound masking efforts included playing tapes of ocean waves, chirping birds, and rustling wind, but this turned out to be distracting. Few people are disturbed by the noise of an air conditioner, a more constant and uniform sound.

Effective sound-masking systems are unobtrusive, constant, and uniform throughout a space. There are many, many ways environment affects behavior. We need to share our experiences so the profession develops this body of knowledge. Awareness as well as technique is important.

Thoughts for the Design Community

1. The client and project come first.
2. The design group as a whole deserves your loyalty, respect and trust. Dedicate yourself to the group.
3. Encourage everyone in the group to be a master of his or her discipline.
4. Learning should be a goal and a pleasure for everyone.
5. Each person should be trained in leadership, treated as a leader and expected to lead when he or she has knowledge or insights others may lack.
6. Talk about and deal with the project in real terms. Don't whitewash or oversimplify, even to yourself.
7. The world constantly changes. We want more than just change. We want to grow with the process.
8. Each short term activity has long term consequences. A system puts short term activities into context. We need a system with which to approach our business.

I am sure you have other thoughts on how to improve our industry.

9

SYSTEM OF THINKING

CHANGE

If we do not grasp change by the hand, it will grasp us by the throat.

WINSTON CHURCHILL

Currently, our world changes at a rate ten times faster than before. The revolutions in thought and a lifetime of experience that once took 50 years now occur in five. Our thinking changed because technology permitted us to do things differently. Business calculators used to cost $3,000 and now cost less than $100. We need a completely different kind of thinking structure to deal with this.

Unexpected change puts companies out of business. Those changes are never what we anticipate. The biggest change in business today is the general environment in which we work. Technology, product availability, management styles, and client expectations demand that we change in response.

The harder you push, the harder the system seems to push back. Systems thinking has a name for this phenomena: compensating feedback. Even well-intentioned intervention causes the system to respond, and this offsets the benefit of the intervention. We all know what it feels like to be faced with this. The more you are trying to improve matters, the more effort seems to be required of you.

Clients want things now, and they expect interior designers to deliver. They expect high quality, and they want to deal with one person, not 50 different vendors. They want that one person to be responsible. Our current system is not set up for this high speed activity. Giving the client what he or she wants is not a smooth and easy process for the designer.

Today we need a structure that will permit interior design to go forward. We define things by the way we understand things to have existed before. This gives us tunnel vision and we can no longer afford it. The world is changing too rapidly. The interior design industry has to change to deal with the massive and revolutionary changes of the recent past. We must change the way we design and our design focus.

Today, the interior design profession is more complex than it was a few years ago, and greatly different from 35 years ago. It involves a knowledge of people and issues of human factors, and expertise in communication skills. This is a great challenge and a great responsibility.

Reengineering has elements that can apply to our industry and the way interior designers work. What really works and what does the client want are still the essential questions. We have to examine every process in the way we work and ask if it is really what the client wants and if it adds value. If it doesn't, get rid of it.

The reality of today's marketplace requires a corporation to be one company worldwide. Likewise, the marketplace demands that the furnishings and design industry operate as a unified entity. Anything less is confusing to the client and ineffective.

Seeking Solutions

Clients expect solutions. They don't want to simply surround themselves with pretty things. They expect answers to their individual design problems, and they expect designers to have the resources to be able to solve their problems. We must know how to handle the casual design dilemmas as well as the very complex. Often, there are issues that no design firm could handle alone, but the client still expects us to link them up to solutions, consultants, and methods. They come to us and expect the whole matter to be resolved, whether the problem is simple or sophisticated.

In the field of psychology, therapy is solution-based and less analytical today. Psychologists feel that what caused the problem is less important than working out a solution. In our industry, I want to know if the present process is good enough to improve. If not, should it be replaced with new processes? What I am talking about is designing a solution, a new way to work, and making it happen.

How do we find the solution? We need to know the rules and how to break them. Today we assume that specialization is necessary. But does the client need specialists? If they just want to paint a wall, do they need a full analysis?

How much of the existing system can we eliminate and still have an effective structure?

We are looking at forming teams of different specialists who can attack the problem and create the solution very effectively—not the traditional chain of command. This team is made up of knowledgeable people, each of whom is capable of making informed decisions. Technology has given us a shared information base.

Technology

Many design products, including lighting fixtures, are manufactured by computer-aided manufacturing (CAM). CAM does at least part of the product testing and development cycle. It lets many engineers work on the same design at the same time, and eliminates endless rounds of review meetings. Within five to ten years many manufacturers will improve the link between design engineering and their manufacturing engineering with CAM technology.

Technology should be used strategically to fit individual needs. It permits us to do much more than any single person can do alone. Sophisticated accounting is possible, for people who are not mathematically inclined, with a simple PC and the appropriate software. Today, businesses are reorganizing and structuring systems to use technology, rather than organizing the business around a task.

For design businesses, it is important to review the systems in use. Do they give you what you need? We cannot simply look at the technology and marvel at what it produces. People computerize existing bookkeeping systems, but their bookkeeping system may not fit the way they do business today. They could be tracking information that does them no good.

The kind of change I am talking about isn't simply restructuring or downsizing—doing more with less. That is not the objective. Reorganization is a process structure; you can simply reorganize what you have. It may be that only part of what you have will work.

We must use technology creatively. A basic PC and a modem give us access to all sorts of information and resources. In general administrative matters, technology often means being able to do more things with greater accuracy and fewer people. There is less need for data-entry people, as each person contributes to the team's decisions and changes.

We don't need as many checks and controls as before. Technology does the checking for us. For years I loved to do spreadsheets, but if you made one mistake, or you changed one thing in one column but didn't do it in another, the whole thing was thrown off. Computer programs make all the changes for us. It's automatic, fast, and there are fewer mistakes. Although someone has to make sure the result are right, we don't have to check every single detail as we did before. We get a high quality product with assured consistency.

Why Do We Do What We Do?

We are looking at performing our processes in an order that flows naturally rather than in an order based on chain of command, documentation procedures, or past performance.

Even though I have written books on business practices, and in my office we still use many of the same systems and techniques I wrote about, I have challenged everyone who works for me to look at the processes. Is there a duplication of effort? Since so much is being done on the computer, certain things done by hand are no longer needed.

Let's look at how we can produce the highest quality work with the most effective price and with whatever makes the most sense. A process may have many different versions, which means that you may do something one way and I may it do it the other way. It doesn't matter, as long as we get the same result.

Some projects need different sources and supervision than others. If we know our vendors and have worked with them many times, we have developed standard ways of working and no longer need to spell out details for each other. Mutual knowledge makes it possible to work more effectively together. And computers let us transfer information without errors. We can repeat an action or bit of information without spending time developing it.

Design a project as if one person could do the whole thing, and then see which parts of it can be done by other team members and which parts by technology. Use people who are trained to do many different things and not just one specialized task. They are in a position to really understand the total job, and should be able to bring more to it than a piece worker on a production line. Every member of the team should be trained and educated in multiple processes.

The job site can be anywhere. We aren't tied to one spot by the need for equipment; office equipment is portable. Our consultants and information sources can come from anywhere in the world. Technology makes communication possible in a matter of seconds. Therefore, we can operate equally well in a large city or a small community.

When it makes more sense to perform a certain function on the job site than in the office, it is technologically possible to take the equipment to the job. Moving the "office" to the construction site changes the nature of the work and ties it directly to the people in the field.

I worked on a project with an architect who handled medium-sized projects from his office in a van. He was able to drive his office up to the project, see the problems, and talk to the contractors. Without leaving the site, he could complete the change orders and revise the prints. When he left the site, it was to go to a new job, not to run back to the office and attend to details.

Opportunity to Excel

A single person can control the project and act as the contact between the client and the design team. This person more or less holds the project together and makes sure that all of these other components are included and work together. In this very complex, technological world our clients are looking for one person who can assimilate information from a number of sources and communicate to them what they need to know in language that they can understand. An interior designer should be qualified to judge which information can be adapted to this project. Information can become confusing if it is not properly managed to fit the project.

There is an opportunity for designers to take the responsibility of coordinating a total design project, including the architectural and engineering aspects. The designer-manager may handle the different parts of the discipline, using those specialists who are perhaps in different offices or even in different cities. We can have a world specialist on the team even if he or she is on the other side of the world and never visits the site. Technology permits us to work very accurately and precisely to produce high quality work. There is no need to guess at anything because we can have instant access to the experts with a personal digital assistant or a portable computer and modem.

We have the technology and resources to produce at a higher level of quality. We also have pressure from clients to produce quality, and quickly. We are living a very litigious time, yet some of those risks are smaller because we have access to top level consultants, and documentation and confirmation are faster, easier, and less expensive. Today we can have the very best people as our consultants and we can do work anywhere in the country with top quality standards and top quality materials.

Clients see change everywhere else in the world. They expect it in their homes, and they are ready for it, but in measured doses arranged by a professional who knows them. They also need designers to keep close reins on the project so that everything is coordinated. The average home doesn't contain much that is that different from what was available 50 years ago. The knowledge and the products are accessible to create dramatic changes in the way people live.

The near future is an opportunity to produce at a higher level with top level resources, for a more demanding client than ever before. People's needs as well as their wants are affected by their understanding of what is possible. If we can show them the possibilities of our field, they are going to want them.

Our field must find ways to educate and excite the client with the possibilities of change. Once we show our clients what is available, the business prospects for the field will change.

REDESIGN FROM THE ROOTS UP

We shape our buildings; thereafter, they shape us.

WINSTON CHURCHILL

In redesigning buildings, we often have to start from scratch because the new functions of the building are sufficiently different from those of the previous owner. The project must be treated as an original design, even though we may use some parts of the previous construction and it is technically adaptive reuse. We still work as if it were an all-original project to determine how that reuse fits into the building that it is available.

This is what we need to do now with our design firms and our industry. To determine the direction of change, we need to know our strengths and weaknesses, individually and as a firm.

The interior design industry is in an "elephant dance" situation. James A. Belasco, in *Teaching the Elephant to Dance* (1990), wrote that elephants are trained by chaining them when they are young, so they can walk only a short distance. When it is older, the chain is symbolic; it is not attached to anything. The elephant has been conditioned to only walk a certain distance when it feels that chain. However, if an elephant is in a barn that catches on fire, fear will break the conditioning and allow the elephant to save itself by running out of the barn. Many people feel tied to a traditional structure. Dr. Belasco is telling us that we need to set a fire and create fear to empower change within our industry.

This opportunity for change is really very positive. We won't have to worry about burnout because we will be doing things differently. People burn out from doing things they are not skilled at, not from doing what they've been trained for. Designing change is something we are good at. We should enjoy the challenge of redesigning our industry.

We have to look at the characteristics of design businesses. Most interior designers are self-reliant individuals who are willing to put in a lot of effort when they believe in the result. We also like change.

First we have to understand where we are going and just what we need to do to get there. We have to use our talents and our ingenuity.

In redesigning your design business the first two questions are: Is this really what we need to be doing today, and what is the appropriate process for whatever it is that is needed within today's market?

Why Aren't We More Flexible?

Many design firms are not concerned enough with what the customer needs or considers valuable. This lack of flexibility and the inefficiency of the division of labor process mean many firms are just not making money today. We need to ask why each step and each process is being done, because some of it may be wrong. The administrative structure for many projects is so expensive and time consuming. If we could spend our time on the actual project and let the paperwork alone, projects would go more quickly and be far less expensive for our clients.

Why are so many design companies rigid, sluggish, clumsy, and noncompetitive? Why aren't we as creative as we need to be? A lot of us are overloaded with processes that could be handled by a computer, rather than a designer. You don't have to spend your life chasing paper.

When you redesign your business and our industry, keep in mind three driving forces:

1. Today customers are in charge. Each client counts because there aren't that many of them out there. They have the upper hand.
2. There is a great deal of competition in our field. It is intense, and comes at us from many different directions.
3. You can count on change. Things are changing so rapidly that if we don't focus on a target, a mission, or a goal, we can really get lost.

After World War II, the demand for goods was so great that little else mattered. There was really little demand for high quality service. People wanted products, and interior designers were able to bring good products to people who could not have afforded it before, but these people didn't understand what high quality design service was. They had no previous experience of design services. It was more a question of could we get the merchandise.

Life Cycles and Issues That Affect Them

Before we can talk about creating the process for running a business, we need a general philosophy, a general vision, a mission. This is the strategy of the business. It is based on the type of business, its directions, and its objectives. Otherwise, there is no point in talking about a system. As times change, our strategies need to change as well.

A good business:

1. has the ability to grow.
2. has the opportunity for reasonable profit.
3. gives us a creative challenge.
4. has the opportunity for diversification and change.

Are you in the right business? In 35 years, my business has changed considerably. My clients have changed and the things that I am able to do have changed, because there are different products available. The umbrella term "interior design" describes many different businesses and many different levels of involvement. Design training is used in interior design, product design, facilities work, and selling products, to name a few applications.

Businesses have life cycles.

During the **introductory phase**, you are thinking of strategy and how it will work.

During **growth**, you may sacrifice immediate rewards for greater rewards in the future. Sometimes this means taking all of the profits and energy and applying it to further growth.

A business is said to have reached **maturity** when business is working and profits are up and everything is working beautifully.

Decline is a normal part of every business cycle, and the design industry is now in decline. At one time interior designers earned a great deal of money by selling products. Now we provide more services. Those cycles will change again as new products become available. We may rise through the process where selling merchandise becomes much more profitable and popular.

Some interior design businesses are seasonal. When designers work at the seashore or in a resort area, they know that clients will be there only part of the year. They know what the cycles are and they work around them. I never thought of my business as having a seasonal cycle, but the nasty winter of 1993-1994 showed me very clearly how the weather affects business, not to mention our whole income and profit structure.

Cycles affect the structure of business. The whole list of products that designers sell and the way we sell them has completely changed. This means we should re-evaluate how selling products affects the rest of our business. What else needs adjustment?

Cycles are normal and occur in everything from the economy and interest rates to world events such as the Gulf War. There is an **economic** cycle. Right now, companies and individuals do not want to spend money on their interiors. Corporations have had to lay people off. As a result they are not going to spend large amounts of money on their corporate headquarters. They have to be very conservative, and this affects the interior design business.

There is a **social aspect.** When it becomes inappropriate for people to look opulent, their spaces become very basic and conservative. In a period such as the Reagan years, it became socially acceptable for people to have well-appointed homes and lavish dress, and that was good for the design industry. Right now, the mature market is untapped and eager for attention. There are different design needs than for a family with school-age children. The way children are cared for has changed, and that affects design of residences and daycare centers. Changes in educational facilities create work for the design industry.

Legal issues affect the design industry. ADA regulations require businesses to make buildings more accessible to a broader range of people. These regulations brought business to some design firms, both in assessing whether structural changes needed to be made, and in making necessary changes. Restrictions based on environmental issues are causing a great deal of fear and concern; interior designers now need to make sure that we are not legally responsible for things that we are not able to control, such as the way the chemical components of furnishings interact.

A renewed concern for **nature** affects business. In the 1970s, worry over fuel consumption limited the geographic range of our businesses. We are now designing for environmentally sound houses that take less fuel to heat and are looking for ways to make larger spaces less expensive.

People do not want to live in an area where the **political** atmosphere is uneasy and difficult, and this affects our client base. People will move to regions with fewer taxes or a better social environment. There are other political issues at work, such as legislation to limit the activities of interior designers or to license interior designers.

Technological advances have brought us many new products, and also affect the way we work.

All of these aspects must be considered in your business strategy.

Changes in the Industry

For years, managing growth was the issue. Now growth has flattened and the problem is the total cost of a job. On the whole, our direct costs are down. Furniture can be produced at less expense than ever before. However, soft costs are up in the form of furniture distribution costs and in running an interior design firm. The administrative structure to track and control the project costs more than the real work of making the product or the project.

We are really dealing with a new set of needs that demands that we restructure our businesses, putting the effort and energy into areas where they are needed and handling other tasks by computers. The people assigned to single-task jobs will need to change as their work evolves. The entire interior design industry needs to work very differently than it has in the past.

Technology changed the market for design services. It also changed the way we work, making task-oriented jobs obsolete because many of the processes—bookkeeping, typing, payroll, for instance—can be done better by one person and a computer than they had been by a whole staff.

Our limits have changed. Easy portable access to information and communication means that talented designers are no longer tied to major cities. There was a time when designers who lived in small communities could not accomplish the same level of design work as designers in New York, California, Chicago, or another major market center. Large or complex projects went to outside firms. Today, with technology and communication you can get all the information you need and work any place. Location no longer limits you to certain types of projects.

Our staffing needs have changed. We now need people who know how to use technology, have good people skills, and are knowledgeable in more than one area.

We must ask basic questions. What should business look like today? What should our product look like and how are we going to make it happen? What do we have to do to create that new design?

This doesn't mean you have to throw everything you know out the window. Change is a process and Pareto's 80/20 rule still applies. The Italian economist of the early twentieth century said that we spend 80 percent of our time doing something that is 20 percent of the process and 20 percent of our time on the 80 percent, the most valuable part.

Look at your day. What are you doing that you really need to do that is effective, that directly relates to completing that client's project? What are you doing as a matter of course that does not contribute to the main objective of the project? This is what we need to look at in redesigning a design firm and in the industry. What can be eliminated? How can we change our thinking, habits, and business structures to direct our energies more effectively toward the clients and projects?

In many small companies, management and planning are not major issues. We are looking at issues such as cash flow. Cash flow was generally simple; we took deposits and kept each job within its own structure. The future offers opportunities for flexibility, but processes that work in certain markets will not be as effective in others. Now people starting businesses need greater amounts of money, a much stronger business structure, and links to the right resources to be effective.

Our client base is as important as our consultants. Just as we link with resources to fit our clients, interior designers are going to have to find the right clients to fit individual practices. I believe that we will be able to serve many more types of clients than we did in the past, but I also believe that we are going to have to cater to those clients and to keep them happy.

We used to be able to work from crisis to crisis without taking time to consider where we were and where we should be. Although we spend a lot of energy on designs for clients and even tell our clients how important it is to understand their direction so they won't get themselves into something they can't get out of, we rarely plan for our own firms. We need to look at our firms in the same way we look at each project. Let's plan based on what the situation is today, what the parameters are of this project and how we can get the project completed most effectively.

Interior design is very much a science, not just an art. Running a business is a science. There is a definite structure, there is that challenge and we must meet the demands of every aspect of our businesses. We can't simply wait for the project of the year to walk in the door.

Change the Way You Think

The will to win is important, but the will to be prepared is vital.

JOE PATERNO

Good relations with both clients and resources are the keys to successful design projects and businesses. We must keep and maintain these relationships because they are not easily replaceable. Your shared experiences build a base of knowledge, a basis for communication. If a client or resource knows you and feels that they know you well, the level of trust and the level of design can improve and increase with each project.

Use all the facilities available to you to make sure that relationship stays strong, because we cannot afford to lose even one relationship during our design career today. Designers who do this well have practices built on what seems to be a minimal number of strong clients. One designer friend had a practice based on three major clients for over thirty years, and it was a terrific practice! He did a lot to take care of these clients, and it was very worth his while.

We must change how we think, as well as what we are doing. We must replace old practices with new ones. In *The Winner Within*, Pat Riley says leadership means defining reality. We define reality for clients. They have all these grand ideas, and we come in and say, "This is what you can do and this is what you can't do. This is how it can be done." Many times we walk out of a project because the goals and objectives of the client are so different from what can actually be accomplished. Interior designers take the lead by defining reality for clients. This is what needs to happen within our companies.

Preparation and Research

Interior design work is going to take a lot more preparation and research than ever before. It already does. Clients expect to hear all the details; they are no longer satisfied to be told, "Everything is going to be just fine." We need to back up our judgments with information because this is what people are used to today. They expect more background data, information, and statistics to be available whenever they ask for it.

VALUES

Words such as value, ethics, and judgment can be confusing, because everyone has a different definition.

If the value of a company is the sum of all the values it teaches, thinks, and practices, there is no room for highly individual definitions. All members of a firm should be operating from a very similar set of values. If you lead a firm, clarify your definitions and share them with the other members.

"Mediocrity...is inevitable if the leadership of the organization perceives integrity as something that can be compromised rather than as a guide to help lift and pull the organization toward the future," Joe Batten wrote in a May 1994 article in *Management Review*. Batten is a leadership consultant and has written 14 books on the subject.

Quality is a value. Customers want it, we want to produce it, and a management strategy based on it is Total Quality Management (TQM). Batten says effective TQM demands a Total Quality Culture, "the never-ending quest for greater quality and service in every dimension of the organization. It encompasses the philosophy, central values, and practices of an organization and involves all its people and resources."

Quality depends on people. People change a vision into a reality. Each person who contributes to a project affects its success.

You can't assume that your values are your client's values. You must either redefine value for them by educating them throughout the project, or accept their values as the standard for the project. Combining these two methods is more likely to produce positive results than either one alone.

Our values have had to change in the last five years because our clients' values have changed. At one time interior designers were thought of as a sort of magician. Now clients realize that many products and services are available through other sources. They don't want the repetition that they had before — they want something customized to suit them. This forces designers to work more creatively.

There is a sheet in my office defining our firm's values: how we see our firm, objectives, qualities, and compensation. I hope that reading this book will help you clarify some of your values.

ETHICS

People are talking about ethics as if it is a threat, and with so much fear that it gets in the way. There's nothing frightening about it. In interior design, in business, and in life, an action is ethical when it benefits everyone involved. Business schools teach ethics as a sort of moral absolutism: do the right thing simply because it is right, even if means your company goes under. A lot of people avoid the issue of ethics entirely, simply because a black-and-white moral stand is too high minded to be workable. It takes years to build a productive business and a good client base. Why throw everything you have built out the window for a principle you only partly understand?

To define interior design ethics we have to clearly define our profession, our own specialties, and the process by which we make interior design happen. Ethics is based on good business practices. Business practice is the system for coordinating the interaction among client and design source. Since you cannot consider any part of a project without it, business practices should be the core of every design curriculum.

To me, the definition of ethics is that everybody wins. Clients must receive a project of value in exchange for their investments. Designers must be appropriately compensated for their efforts, whether the compensation is money, publicity, or other forms of payment. And the sources — contractors and materials resources— must receive adequate compensation for the quality of their labor and merchandise. **Ethics includes a respect for all the participants in the project.**

It is our responsibility to see that our firms earn an appropriate income, that our employees are properly compensated, and that they have the right tools to work with, whether the tools are equipment or training. These are ethical responsibilities

I'm not in favor of designers becoming martyrs and giving people something for nothing just because that makes the designer a better person. Even better people have to eat.

The financial part of our business is an evaluation tool. Our clients can judge how much they want to invest in a project. We use money to pay our staff and sources, to get additional training, and to equip the studios in which we work.

Ethics is simply basic business principles. For interior design, communication that respects the other person and education are the foundation for good business. We build relationships with clients from the first contact through interviews and decision-making. We develop a rapport with our resources, learning about their skills, ability to produce, and capacity of the factory. We study the products to learn the scope of appropriate use. Then we evaluate to match the products and resources to the client's situation, use, and budget.

Thousands of elements can affect our decisions: performance levels, artistic value, what's appropriate for the space, and whether we can make it happen. As much as we might like a design, there are situations in which it's just not possible to use a product. What good is a beautiful product if it is too expensive or if it simply can't be installed?

As designers, we are responsible for reviewing the client's human dimension, for being aware of more than they tell us in words. Take note of how a client acts and moves, how well he or she sees and hears, and how he or she responds to tactile sensations. Some people dislike rough or nubby textures. A person who wears glasses or contact lenses will, at some point, remove them and perform certain tasks without them. The person who drags his or her feet due to a physical limitation is very likely to trip on the edge of that beautiful Oriental rug and fall. Design should allow for these human factors.

I tell my staff every day that it is the designer's responsibility to not kill too many people with our design. We must look at our designs critically to be sure that nothing will injure the people who must use the space. This includes children, older people, visitors who are unfamiliar with the space, people in a hurry, and people who are not quite awake.

It is our responsibility to remain up to date in all areas of design requirements from codes and laws to trends. Our clients do not want the same products that can be found in the local department store or Ikea. They want products specifically chosen for their needs. This may mean custom designed pieces, or it may simply mean using catalog items in new and different ways. Today, our responsibility to our clients means considerable research and study, as well as using consultants.

In interior design we become involved in many aspects of our client's private lives, whether it is a business or residential project. Maintaining the boundaries between designer and client is a critical issue. Show that you appreciate the sensitivity of these issues. If you must open dresser drawers and count items of clothing, ask the client if you may do so, or if he or she would rather do it themselves.

Client confidentiality holds the same obligation for interior designers as it does for physicians and attorneys. You may gain personal information that could harm a marriage. In a business situation, a designer may become part of a plan for a clients' business growth. If the details were to be made public, this could damage the business—to say nothing of the designer/client relationship.

Ethics and respect for boundaries also exists between designer and sources. Our resources may have proprietary methods for making or finishing products. Designers may have developed their own unique ways of doing things. These proprietary techniques may be the basis of their income. There are things clients do not need to know, and there are things designers do not need to know. Clients should understand that the craftsmen working in their spaces need to concentrate on their work. Even though the space belongs to the client, it is the craftsman's workplace.

Throughout the entire design process we have to communicate and learn. If we don't have effective communication, obviously the quality of the design and the quality of the project are in jeopardy and we all lose. When products are used incorrectly, our resources lose. Design firms lose too, because the perceived quality of their design is affected when products they specify don't perform well. That project won't generate new business. And of course the client is the big loser because the client hasn't gotten the very best that could be produced by the practice of interior design.

With some people good communication is impossible; there is a strong likelihood for fatal misunderstandings. In my experience, there are no lawsuits where there is good communication. It is the designer's ethical responsibility not to take on a client with whom he or she cannot communicate well, or to discontinue service after becoming aware of the poor match of client and designer.

Today the word ethics is overused. You hear and read "ethics" so much today that it becomes a threat. You begin to doubt your internal definition of the word. Isn't ethics just common courtesy and sound business practice? Robert Fulghum's claim that he learned everything he needed to know in kindergarten has a lot of truth in it. Play fair, share everything, don't hit people, clean up your own messes, and say you're sorry when you hurt someone.

If a project, and a relationship with a client, is set up to respect all parties, and it's managed so that all parties benefit, that is ethics.

ETHICAL PURPOSE

Businesses must have a purpose that is more than the bottom line. It has become the style to have commandments. In the interior design field, the commandments are:

1. To give service to our clients in the best possible way. To bring to them all of the different products and services that are required for their different projects. To give them quality services beyond their expectations.

2. To give our clients value. Whatever dollar amount they spend, see that they have value for it. Make sure that they get the best possible job for their investment.

3. To bring home a reasonable profit to pay for our resources and compensate our employees appropriately.

We can't gain our entire incomes from a single project. We need standards for charging that are good, fair, and simple. It isn't ethical to charge more than normal just because you believe the client won't know the difference. I want to give my clients the best project I can for the best possible dollar amount. I know that to keep clients over the long term, I have to offer them quality and honest service. When we manage to save money on items, we pass along the savings to the client.

Our firm's mission statement is to provide the best possible design service to our clients and to give them the opportunity, through interior design, to enhance their lives to the highest level that can be gained through designing an environment. We want to keep our clients for life and we want to help develop their opportunities in life.

Johnson & Johnson's credo is famous:

1. Service to its customers
2. Service to its employees and management
3. Service to the community
4. Service to its stockholders

This is why it responded to a rash of product tampering that resulted in deaths by recalling the product, devising more tamper-proof seals, and embarking on a public relations campaign that stressed the reliability of the product. There was no other possible way for the firm to react because they knew what had to be done. The experts had predicted that the brand was dead, based on the loss of trust the murders had inspired. And the public responded with what marketing experts at the time called a miracle.

RESPONSIBILITY

To have a strong practice based on what clients need and want, interior designers will have to assume much more responsibility on projects. This goes against legal advice to limit design liability, but I have noticed that the designers who get work and who will continue to get work are those who are truly responsible for the project. Today people are willing to pay for assured results. They don't want to buy something that has loopholes and ifs.

Each period brings with it different responsibilities. Today's clients want the designer to be responsible for the total job and don't care how it happens, even though they want to be part of the decision-making process. They know enough about interior design to realize that it's full of potential for making bad judgments and that they cannot complete the project with the level of skill and quality they desire with any degree of ease. They know that working with a designer will expand their range of choices and the level of quality for the project. They want you to make the environment they discussed with you a reality.

Assuming the responsibility while limiting the risk means accepting projects you know your firm can bring to a successful completion. This is important in selecting new projects. Don't do it unless you are sure that you can complete it with reasonable ease and without being overly concerned with the liability issues. There is no such a thing as a contract that will truly protect you from problems or from being sued. The only real protection is experience and a confidence in the extended team of vendors and contractors.

Contracts are necessary. They are as important to our system as bonds and certificates of insurance. Contracts are a part of clear communication, but they can't protect us from choosing the wrong client or the wrong product, or a breakdown in the designer-client relationship, and these are the real reason designers get sued. If you are so afraid that you feel you need contracts spelling out who is responsible for what to protect you, probably this is not the right contract or client for you.

According to Manny Steinfeld of Shelby Williams, there has not been a single lawsuit against a designer or manufacturer in the United States in which the designer or manufacturer ever won in court. The times are not right for this.

Accounting for your results and assuming responsibility are at the core of Total Quality Management, Employee Empowerment, Customer Satisfaction, and most other popular programs of business management. Nothing will work as well as it should if people won't accept personal accountability for their own actions.

In his book *The Oz Principle*, Craig Hickman sets forth four basics of constructive change. The first is to recognize reality for what it is. Next, own it. You may not have created the problem, but you are part of it. Accept it and go on from there. Solving the situation is the third step. Instead of saying "Why me," just go on and plan your solution. Finally, do it. Put your plan into action.

The responsibility for handling a design project should rest with the designer. Working with vendors and craftspeople you know and whose quality of work you know decreases your actual risk. When you share a project with other very knowledgeable consultants and vendors, you also share the responsibilities with them. The blaming and the adversarial relationship that used to go on, that was accepted and even expected among designers, contractors, and vendors, is not acceptable any more. Clients don't want to hear why it didn't work. They want to know what you are going to do to make it right.

When you take on a project, give the clients what they want, or something a bit better than what they want. Don't try to make the project too perfect. Sometimes we take on projects and try for things too far beyond what the clients asked for—and that's where we get into trouble. I'm sure we all have done this at one time or another. Our goal is quality products and service built on relationships. There is no need to blame anyone when the relationships are good and you communicate well and often. Clients don't want surprises.

Today we have the technology and the resources to take better control of a project. Faxes and computer modems give all the key players the same information. Technology has taken some of the mystery out of our work by giving us wider access to information, but we are still dependent on the quality of the information.

Most firms are leaner than in the 1980s. Staff has to be targeted to meet the demands of the present market. A company must have a consistent core of key players and still be flexible enough to accommodate bringing in consultants specific to a project. This gives us an opportunity to bring in high level staff who are not necessarily on our payroll but still a part of our company. Communications technology enables us to consult with people who may never actually visit the site. We can send photos and videos of a site to consultants on the other side of the world to get an informed opinion. Craftspeople can be at work within minutes instead of weeks.

Know your vendors and craftspeople. Because security and safety are major concerns for our clients, they become major concerns for us. It is our responsibility to monitor the people that we send into each project. In a recent *Trend Letter*, John Naisbitt wrote that over five percent of the people working as nursing home aides have criminal records. How much do you know about the background of the carpet-layers, electricians, and vendors working with you on projects? This is an area in which we will have to be much more cautious.

JUDGMENT

Judgment is an essential quality for designers to have and to nourish. We use judgment to sift through the many sources of products and information to design a project and make it a reality. The design process continually adds to our experience, providing clear and visible outcomes to each exercise of judgment. Good judgment requires one to be aware of the context, to make accurate evaluations and interpretations, and to be able to generalize beyond the moment.

Judgment may involve the critical evaluation of a person, product, space or situation. It includes matching available products to the clients' needs, values and directions. It also includes the process of appreciation, comparison, and appraisal of values, often expressed in the form of an attitude. Good judgment involves an accurate awareness of the meaning of cues and stimuli. Judgment requires one to be able to make accurate discriminations, to be able to weigh risks and benefits, and to anticipate events so there is an accurate appraisal.

Poor judgment is a misreading of the cues, and this results in an unwanted outcome. If the person is unable to weigh the impact of an event, then he or she is likely to show poor judgment. If an interior designer fails to consider the effect of a new color element on the colors already in a space, this poor judgment may negatively affect every item in the room.

There is definitely an element of intuition in good judgment.

VISION AND PURPOSE

Most adults have little sense of vision. We have goals and objectives, but these are not vision. Vision is a specific destination, a picture of a desired future. Vision without purpose is not a good idea.

Ron Fritz says, "It is not what the vision is, it's what the vision does. Truly creative people use the gap between visions and current reality to generate energy for change."

Vision establishes direction. Purpose is the reason that an organization exists. This includes short- and long-term objectives, but purpose reflects the core values of the organization.

One purpose of a design firm might be to design great interior spaces that change and develop the opportunities of our clients, and, through this, to give our staff an opportunity to express and use their talents.

Vision is knowing something has to be done. There is no option; it just must be done. We need to build a shared vision among the home furnishings and design industry, but individuals have to develop their own visions before they can be shared.

People don't think of themselves as visionaries, but they may be called visionaries. If you can communicate your vision so that other people become excited and passionate about becoming part of the team to carry out this great endeavor, then you have one of the requirements of being a leader.

Designers are born visionaries. We have an internal obsession to create. There is such a great need today for design vision. We just need to put it into a system and to be able to communicate it.

POWER

What is power? The best definition I have found is that power is the ability to get things done. That includes being able to put together the right people and the right resources and accomplish your goal.

Today, power results principally from relationships. Whether it is marketing, management, or leadership, everything is based on the style of relationships. Many relationships that used to work for the interior design industry do not work today. The strongest companies are built on who you know and whether you can match the right person with the right project.

Information is power. Being able to locate the right information is a demonstration of power, whether it comes from resources, consultants, other craftsman, networked information resources, your library and files, the encyclopedia in your office or whatever you have that builds your base of information. A Harvard professor of business administration, Howard H. Stevenson, says "To be powerful, you must be able to compute your value in the marketplace you want to conquer, change the estimate that market places on your value, and convince that market of the value of your assets, services or products."

Power comes from understanding what your range of knowledge is, and working within it. You can expand what you know, but you should work within the realm of what you know. One can be a generalist in what you know but professionally interior designers must become specialists. Every field—law, medicine, interior design—has become so complex that no single person can claim to know all there is to know about his or her field.

You may have exposure to the law where it touches interior design, but as a designer you wouldn't practice interior design law. We may have a basic understanding of many design specialties—teleconferencing, interior plantscaping, or construction management, for instance—because we have worked with those specialists on several occasions. This doesn't substitute for training and experience. It would be unprofessional, almost dishonest to claim that a single person or small firm can handle everything in house. Do a reality check on your firm. Who are you, what do you know, and can you work within those boundaries? Focus is the most important discipline. Look at the star performers in interior design and other fields. Each person focused on the needs of the time and the needs of their client, and devised a way to meet those needs.

Designers are visionaries, but power is more than the ability to have visions. You have to be able to carry it out, to turn your vision into reality. Presenting a concept that you cannot produce at an acceptable level of quality erodes your professional position. Don't present a design you cannot produce well.

In today's market, it's really very dangerous to seem too powerful. It's the people who are most visible who get into trouble. Politicians have been absolutely destroyed by media exposure of some incident in their lives. How you use your power is important.

Maybe the outdated concept of designer as a master of the unknown has backfired, and is part of the reason the industry is in chaos. Initially clients were loyal because they believed they could not get products that well made anywhere but through designers. Now good design and quality products are absolutely everywhere. There are opportunities to buy the well-made and unusual through catalogs, museum stores, discount stores, and 800 telephone numbers.

But a large choice is also confusing and exhausting. Designers who are able to take the mass of information and show clients how to discriminate and what to use where are needed.

Recently, a client asked me about a decision on her project that would have to be made, and I told her that decision would be made after we made the first two. She said, "You know, I think that's the thing I appreciate most about this relationship; the fact that you put things in order, so I'm not stressing out over making a decision that I don't know enough about to make comfortably."

Part of the power of designer-client relationship is in the ability to put making decisions about furniture and furnishings into a context that makes the decision-making exciting, positive, and reasonably easy for the client.

Somebody somewhere commented that if something is really interesting, it's probably not worth much. Think of all the hours we can spend talking about the idiosyncracies of clients, designers, and life in general. It *is* interesting and even fascinating, but is it really important? Some products are presented with a very large promotional and advertising program, but the presentations don't give us what we need to know about a piece of furniture or a product. We have to look at the constants—not what is interesting or fun, but what really works.

We used to say that a person was as valuable as his Rolodex. Today, perhaps we are as valuable as our modem connections and access to information systems. Interior design is the system that enables us to bring this information and products to clients. You can't run a design studio without good information. You can have the most beautiful space look beautiful filled with wonderful objects, but what do those things represent? Are they the things you need to complete your projects?

Do you truly understand your limitations? Your design history should show you both limitations and opportunities, and this knowledge is strength. We can use the technique of concession, and tell clients that there are some areas in which our skills are not as good as in other areas. Stress the strengths, but admit the limitations. This keeps you from taking on projects that will require too much learning as you go along.

The strongest designs are not always those associated with a specific style, period, or particular designer. The strongest designs arise from meeting the needs of a given situation. It's a matter of how well the designer investigated the needs of the client, and how well the resulting space and furnishings meet those needs. When a designer does this well, the design raises the client's standard of living or brings greater opportunity.

ATTRIBUTES OF A POWERFUL ORGANIZATION

A powerful organization doesn't have rigid, top-down management. Instead, it has a strong sense of mission that all employees have been educated to share. The leaders of these organizations know how to bring a team together, and they realize that without a team, you don't have anything.

Being a good architect of time is an example of power. Planning time is just as important as planning space. It requires just as much input and just as much thought, and can shape the way you do business, just as environments affect the way we behave. You create one that works and helps you or you are constantly fighting time.

Who you know is one element of power. Very few people have become accomplished in a major art or profession without a patron or a backer.

Whether it is large or small, a powerful firm has good support, often provided by an advisory board or a single person. An advisory board does not have the same responsibility as an official board of the corporation; usually there is no liability. The board is made up of people who can help, by introducing you to the right person, or by teaching you what they know about the field. Good members of an advisory board include suppliers, the past owner of the firm, or someone who knows you and understands the field. An advisory board is a powerful resource, on call but not constantly present.

Traditionally, a powerful person was one who gave orders. Today a powerful person is one with the ability to orchestrate profitable change.

You can develop a powerful firm through developing your staff: you want them to experience a wealth of opportunities and a wealth of action. Arthur Gensler, who heads the largest interior design firm in the nation, says he has succeeded by hiring people who are smarter than he is. Hiring people who can challenge you increases your strength, and it makes people think you are stronger and smarter than you may actually be.

Power by intimidation is not where design challenge and excitement is today, even though intimidation seems built into power. Clients are afraid that they will make the wrong decision. They are afraid that they don't know the right people, the right contractors, the right products, and that they don't have the skills that you have. Your knowledge is intimidating.

Power is concentration, meditation, and listening effectively to the people that you are communicating with.

Power can be developed through marketing. You can have the greatest power and the greatest abilities, but if no one knows about it, it won't do you any good. And marketing is relationships.

Marketing is courting your potential partner. It is based on getting to know each other, and developing the client's confidence in your abilities. This is the kind of marketing that works best for interior designers, because the knowledge we gain in working with a client can be quite intimate. We must understand what motivates people to buy. Young people may simply need furniture to sit on because they have none. The older person who is artistic may be looking for art furniture, something really unusual, stimulating, exciting, and attractive. You can't market to a group if you do not understand what motivates them to buy.

Today a top designer is a person capable of creating items of intellectual property, things different and exclusive to their practice. Anyone can come up with one or two or even five good ideas. A top designer may not have the time to make real even 15 percent of what he or she designs. Second, a top designer knows how to inspire and empower people to be productive. *These two things are extremely important in a highly capable designer.*

IMAGE

What do people think of when they hear "interior design"? Peter Senge discusses this in *The Fifth Discipline*. Is our image the one shown in the television program *Designing Women?* On the show, the business of design took a back seat to the personal relationships of the women. Television programs on the medical profession, such as *Marcus Welby, M.D.* and *Dr. Kildare*, romanticized the profession and the personal relationships were flavoring to add validity.

Even when the presentation of an interior designer is not intended to be the literal truth, it affects the way designers can work because it colors what people think about the profession. Maybe we need someone to write scripts for us. Perhaps Alby Phibbs (the past president of ASID who said that his role was to be a cheerleader for the profession) can pull out some of his great material and show us how to present the designer in a Marcus Welby style, as people who should be respected for their knowledge and abilities, yet still people with human failings.

Dressing for power now means dressing for action. Now, the Ford Motors board is photographed in windbreaker jackets. In Operation Desert Storm, General Schwartzkopf led the troops wearing fatigues just like everyone else. Today, I'm wondering whether the dress of our field is appropriate. In my own studio, I'm leaning toward a style that makes it seem as though we are not afraid to get dirty, something like an artist's smock or a lab coat.

Opulence is really out of style when it comes to working today. The three-piece suit and the plush corner office is not the way heads of corporations want to be seen. They want to be seen as part of the gang, part of the working group. We are now talking about working managers, people that are not afraid to get their hands dirty. We have to look at our studios, the location, the moods they set, and many other issues. Are they too opulent, and do they make people feel uncomfortable?

Our clients today are very bright. They see, they know, they understand. They have been exposed to our field and they may know more about some aspects of it than we do. We need to acknowledge this in every contact we have with clients. Our presentations should concede their knowledge and go on from there.

Concession can give an appearance of strength. Sometimes we need to acknowledge that we have failed, that something did not work, that there was a mistake. By always seeming all-knowing and trying to make everything right, we create a false image of our field. We need to be honest with ourselves and say this works and this doesn't and this is why. I often tried to protect myself, my firm, and my staff by saying, "Oh, we'll take care of that, no problem." When there is a problem, it is better to acknowledge it, and then find an appropriate way of fixing it.

What's your visual image? Your letters, drawings, graphics— any interaction that involves the visual—can become dated. We ought to redo our graphics every few years, and the same is true for the furnishings in our studios. Some things do last for a very long time, but we need different textiles or other adaptations.

Every document you send out should look professional. There are ways to format documents on the computer to give them visual appeal. Sometimes all you have to do it to copy the work onto an attractive piece of paper.

IT'S HARD TO CHANGE YOUR SYSTEM OF THINKING

At a recent seminar I led on the changes in our business, we broke into teams to discuss the problems of making a company grow in a period of rapid technological and social development.

One small contract design firm specializing in medical centers and hospitals saw itself as being in competition with some of the largest design firms in this specialty. The CEO of the company asked the group to suggest ways to make her firm more competitive with these large firms.

We all agreed that the one thing she needed before she could consider moving into this larger arena was at least one more person in her firm who was equally as qualified as she was. This person would have about the same level of education and experience and who could, when the CEO was out doing marketing or client development work, make everything run well back at the office.

How do you find a person like this? I asked her what her first step would be. She replied that she would put an ad in the newspaper, perhaps in one of the interior design magazines, or the ASID Report. The ad would be for a *project manager*.

"Wait a minute!" I said. "Would you want to work for me or anyone here as a project manager? Of course not. Then why would you expect the caliber of person that you want, someone who is your equal, to come to work for you as a project manager?"

We convinced her that hiring a project manager was not the answer. When you add an equal to your firm, you have to think about what this level of person would want, and it's not a project manager's job. He or she would want to be your partner, co-owner, or in some way a key player. There are several ways to structure this relationship formally. The most important thing is to treat the person as if he or she is equal in responsibility and authority.

It is interesting that even when we know that we have to do things differently to acquire and succeed in this rapidly changing market, we think in terms of the traditional system. It's hard to break habit patterns. Business theories keep telling us to drop the hierarchical process, to empower individuals to be more responsible for what they do, to hire people with greater skills and abilities and more independence to run our firms correctly. But we still think in terms of hierarchy. We still think the old way.

In the new system of thinking, we must consider how people want to work. The questions to ask are why it benefits you or the person you are considering hiring to join your firm. Maybe you should be merging two firms. Would that give you both an advantage? It is important that there be advantages for both parties.

A firm's value and potential may not be where it should be because the wrong person was hired, or brought in under the wrong parameters.

You have to be honest with clients and potential staff from the beginning. There is nothing about your company that anyone with reasonable intelligence and contacts cannot find out. There are no secrets. There was a day when the owner of a company kept the books away from everyone else and no one knew what he or she made. But that's not true today. Almost everyone knows exactly what you make. In that case it needs to be a very fair program because once this knowledge is out no one is comfortable with a firm that isn't very honest and very forthright.

Changing your system of thinking takes experience after experience and constant reminders. You need to learn to think, to visualize and to develop your company using a new system of thinking, because without the right kind of thinking you will not perform properly. It takes a coach, a constant tutor, and all types of reminders on a regular basis to learn to change.

Who do you want to work with? What conditions would that person want as part of the agreement? How will this work with the rest of the people who make up the firm? Is your current program one that will bring you the future you want? Are these the kind of people you want to spend your time with?

This is just as serious as selecting a marriage partner, because a good relationship should last for a very long time. We spend a lot of time with the people that we work with—sometimes much more time than we do with a spouse.

Hot Markets for Small Companies

1. Health care

2. Exporting

3. Education and training

4. Environmental products and/or services

5. Children and seniors

SOURCE: *Home Office Computing,* May 1994.

10

LEARNING PROGRAM

KEEP ON LEARNING

There is a gap between interior design practice, education, and industry.

It used to take 50 years for information to become obsolete. Now it happens in less than five years. University professors are required to spend a minimum of one day a week researching their fields. We are in the same situation. Interior designers cannot afford to spend less than one solid day per week keeping up with issues related to design.

In interior design, every day, we are in situations in which we want more knowledge! Is there an easy format for people to replace that knowledge?

It isn't practical nor is it really effective to force all interior designers back into the universities after they've been practicing for five years, to spend another five years relearning the discipline. Experience is a great teacher, but experience alone is not enough. We need to bring new techniques to our practices if we are to elevate the quality of our work and keep up with today's clients.

We learn by doing and by testing, which is why some teaching methods have changed so drastically. In the 1940s and 1950s, children were told to memorize. Now, very often the teacher lets the students explain subjects to each other, and gives them opportunities to learn by doing.

Have we really mastered our discipline? I think that the more you learn, the more you realize how much there is still to learn.

Some of the most successful people in every field are the most dedicated students.

Education should not stop when you receive a certificate or a diploma. I have always spent at least 20 hours a week educating myself by spending time with consultants, reading business and design publications, and taking short courses. Interior design is a very important part of my life and I enjoy pursuing new information.

According to *Fortune* magazine, the most successful corporations of the 1990s will be learning organizations. Success is based on the ability to learn faster than your competitors.

Continuing education should be part of every employment agreement. A certain amount of time and money will be dedicated to continuing education, and the expense in time and money should be shared by employer and employee.

Every industry needs to revamp its curriculum. In 1994, the big three auto makers told universities to stop turning out traditional engineers. They want engineers with people skills. Automaker Dennis Pawley says that when he talks to students at MIT, he probably turns off thirty percent of them by describing the work. "But that's okay. I don't want them working for me."

Why We Need to Keep Learning

Handing clients prepackaged solutions doesn't work today. They know it. Sometimes they feel they can do it better themselves. Technology means we are only five steps ahead of our clients in knowledge. We have to keep learning so we can stay the necessary twenty steps ahead.

Learning increases our abilities. Some organizations are spending as much as 40 percent of their time training people. I believe that encouraging people to learn is a major responsibility for any organization today. We must help each person within the group develop his or her own talents and abilities so that each individual can bring to that organization the very best. Companies and leaders should stop trying to control people, and instead develop and encourage them.

Passing certain tests or attaining certain credentials in interior design does not mean a person is actually qualified to deal with all problems. Once we head our own firms or become designers, we think we've arrived! *We have not arrived.* We really have to start all over again because the challenges and opportunities are new and different.

When we were in school, no one ever imagined many of the problems common today. Some of the information we learned is now useless, but the *process* is valuable. Fortunately we were trained to deal with constant change. Every day we start all over again, but it is not a blank slate. Your knowledge base is everything that happened yesterday.

People learn from experience, but after you've been designing for a long time, does every day actually increase your knowledge or have you simply repeated your first year 20 times? It's time to look at our practices and ask how many different kinds of experiences we have had.

So much in our industry repeats some standard form given us by a manufacturer. True, it's a great design, but is this product really needed for that situation? We really have to reexamine our design efforts. Are we keeping up with the times or using the same old things in the same old ways? Are our clients offered the opportunity for the top level design—design worthy of this time? Is our industry unwilling to consider that some of the issues brought up by clients really *are* different from things we've handled before and therefore require different solutions?

So much in our industry is proprietary knowledge. The crafts workrooms so necessary to the quality of our work don't want people to learn from them, but a certain amount of information must be shared to ensure the quality of the work. An atmosphere that supported shared knowledge would require the different crafts to explain things in words designers understand. This has to result in a better product for the crafts and the designers.

Tom Frank, ASID, helped decorate windows in his father's store when he was 14. Working to pay for his design education, he learned plumbing, electrical work, welding, cement finishing, and carpentry. If there is a question about any of his instructions, he can show the crew exactly what he wants.

How can we know what to ask for when we have limited experience of what is possible? A period of work in a craft related to the design industry will deepen any student's understanding and make him or her a better designer. Our field does not have programs that encourage designers to learn crafts, and it should.

Sharing Knowledge Unifies Groups

Just as the world expects a global company to have the same standards and practices throughout its many factories, the market of potential consumers of home furnishings and design services needs the industry to be unified. Education is one way to go about it.

AMP, a Fortune 500 company based in Harrisburg, Pennsylvania, has a training program that communicates what the internal experts know. Before the company invested in its human resource base, the company lost valuable expertise as some of its experts retired, and standards varied between departments and facilities. Now an internal education coalition writes down the knowledge of the experts for use as future reference.

The firm designs and manufactures connectors for the electrical and electronics industries. To maintain its leadership in the marketplace and to maintain product excellence, the firm uses real-world case studies and AMP language while teaching courses. The student manuals and class notes serve as "cookbooks" (recipes or patterns on which new creativity is based). AMP engineers don't have to reinvent the wheel each time they want to use it.

Designers have a similar need to write down and share what we already know. This sharing of knowledge will wear away some of the barriers to communication that have made the design industry appear so fragmented to outsiders. AMP called in university professors with a minimum of 15 years experience to work with its internal experts in developing the courses. Our professional organizations, educational institutions, and industry resources should work together to create courses of education. Doing so will help strengthen our ties to each other, and this bonding will strengthen the industry as a whole.

For years design firms have blamed industry problems on an outside enemy responsible for taking their business away. Our major problem is within. Once we recreate our field as one in which continual mutual learning by the designer, the client, and the industry is part of the excitement, we can return the design field to one in which designers actually accomplish the challenging things that they came into this field to do.

Designers Teach Clients

Enhancing information for our clients is part of our role as designers. It is our responsibility to make sure that the client, whether it is a person trying to direct community activity by a community center, the manager of a sizable business, or a person redoing a living room, understands what the elements of the design will do.

It is our responsibility to explain the environmental effects of interior design in ways that have meaning for our clients. For example:

This color scheme is going to excite.

This color scheme is going to be warm, quiet, subtle.

This color scheme, because it has a gray base, is not good to use among older people because older people see blues as gray. So maybe we need to make our colors a bit clearer or brighter, or use more contrast.

Our clients need to understand that color choices are not random and arbitrary and based on whim or fashion. We need to convey that color looks different to a 20-year-old person than to a person who is 60 or 70. Each new item you introduce changes the perception of color for every other item.

This type of information is available in medical texts as well as essays on the effects of aging. We can supplement what we learn from texts on color for the artist with sociological and anthropological information. We respond to colors differently just because we were born in certain cultures. Here we wear white wedding dresses.

In the Orient, white is a funereal color, and wedding dresses are black or red.

From culture to culture, from area to area, human reactions to space and color differ. Anthropologist Edward T. Hall named the study of this phenomenon "proxemics," the physical, psychological, and cultural impact of space on people.

What Should We Know?

Interior design programs are great at teaching the problem-solving process, but don't go far enough in teaching communication skills. Students are trained to design offices, and they do it well. The truth of it is that there aren't as many offices to design as there used to be, and there are many other things designers ought to be doing. Today interior design education needs more emphasis on the science and research aspects of interior design.

We ought to learn how to develop residential spaces that truly change people's lives. We ought to be trained to create new styles of community centers. We ought to be trained to create environments that support and enhance the way people work, move, and interact. Information on how to design to work with peoples' emotions exists; it is called environmental psychology. Sociologist Robert Sommer and Christopher Alexander wrote about it in the 1960s and 1970s.

Designers do not want standard, routine work; stability; and minimal changes. We want meaningful change. Interior design education teaches us that every day there will be a new problem. This experience is perhaps one of the greatest assets we have in dealing with the challenges of today.

The world needs so much that there are plenty of meaningful changes. The challenge today is to improve the lifestyle of every person, both within the work environment and at home. This is our mission for the day.

We have the tools to do this in ways no other profession can. We have to reorganize our profession to move forward. We must stop looking to outsiders for answers. Our answer will come from looking at our own abilities and designing a field that meets real needs.

REDESIGNING AN INTERIOR DESIGN EDUCATION

The present continuing education system is not enough. My practice is changing almost daily. I need information and education in subjects that didn't exist when I got my training. This information must come from a neutral, noncompetitive information source with high standards, not solely from a company generating a product it wants to sell, and *not* from a networking system of possibly competitive design firms.

Education Today

A formal interior design education is a four- to five- year program in a FIDER accredited college or university. FIDER recommends that one-third of design education should be through formal education, one-third through professional organizations, and one-third through industry. Either during or immediately after that program, the design student serves a practicum (period of assigned fieldwork) or an internship with an accredited design firm. This is usually followed by beginning work as a junior designer for a professional design firm, with the junior member doing documentation, design development, drafting, and general support work for the experienced interior designer.

Practicing interior designers can get specialized training in the form of Continuing Education Units, or CEUs, given by professional design organizations such as the American Society of Interior Designers (ASID) and the International Interior Design Association (IIDA). CEUs are also offered through universities such as Harvard, UCLA, Parsons, Pratt and others. Some programs require on-campus time from a day to a week. More intensive on-campus training is afforded by master's degrees and Ph.D.s. Some designers have returned to school to take undergraduate courses that were not offered when they were in school.

CEUs bring education directly to the local design center or chapter level so designers don't need to take large blocks of time from their practices, but there are drawbacks. Today's CEU programs vary greatly in academic level and according to the instructor. Design associations are successful at organizing and administering the programs, but there is no mechanism for evaluation for either the programs or the skill level of the designer taking the programs. Whereas for design schools, a FIDER accreditation pretty much guarantees that the design education will cover the essentials and may include some specialties.

For CEUs to be a reliable and effective way to update our educations, we need a viable rating system for courses and students.

Time Works Against Us

Rapid change has made the education of even recent graduates, let alone that of anyone who has been practicing for more than five years, obsolete. We need to be reeducated as we practice. For some designers, reeducation is essential because their specialty no longer exists or is no longer salable. There are new regulations, advances that complement what we already know, and specialties that are unfamiliar. Most interior designers are probably somewhat behind on or uncomfortable with one or more issues that affect their practice.

Continuing education is a critical need for people in any business. We need access to new information and ideas daily, just to maintain our interest levels and our ability to create. The question is how to get that education while working in the field. Many designers are already committed to a position or to their own companies, and therefore cannot take off a year or two to get advanced and specialized training. We need a more practical and economical way to acquire educational updates.

We have a glut of information, but there is no easy, accessible, and organized source of information. It appears almost a paragraph at a time, in general business newspapers, in the journals of fields allied to design, in engineering journals, and on Internet on other computer access services. It also comes from day-to-day practice. Sometimes sifting through the information to find what is usable is too big a job. To keep abreast of changes in the design field, interior design professionals currently must leave their practices and go to a university for a block of time. And even if they spend months each year on reeducation, they won't get all the information needed because it is not in any one location.

A university professor, Dr. Arnold Lazarus, says he is able to keep current in his field because he is blessed with "very bright, inquisitive students who read widely, ask questions and then get me scurrying off to find answers and sources I might never even have thought about without their input."

Lazarus further states that workshops can be expensive and time-consuming, and that he cannot rely solely on professional journals for up-to-date information, because what people are willing to commit to writing "is not very illuminating." Dr. Lazarus is a clinical psychologist as well as a university professor. It is reasonable to assume that "illuminating" articles are equally few and far between in other professions. Interior design is no exception.

Fewer Opportunities for On-the-Job Training

The secondary problem is that many designers no longer need a support person, and that curtails the training a young designer can acquire. Formerly, students who graduated from college came into the workplace with good drafting and rendering skills and with aptitudes to support practicing interior design professionals.

Economics, technology, and the level of complexity of design work mean that design firms often don't need junior members to the degree they used to. Mid-level staff members, who used to take the responsibility for training their juniors, have been replaced by technology or eliminated. With fewer people in the firm, it is less and less possible to train junior staff members, because doing so can lower productivity. This means the requirements for an *entry level* designer have changed.

Design students say they learn more from actual practice than from all their classes and bookwork. They show more and more interest in learning the basics of running a business. Design educator Nick Politis says that probably only half of what designers need to know is learned in the classroom, and the other half is learned on the job. It is important for both the design student and design education system to revise their models or there will be many misplaced or disappointed people.

Jack Fields, head of Edward Fields Carpets, says today's designers are taught the mechanics of design, and that most people who are trained only in the mechanics of interior design have no basic concept of design. Design is inborn and gets developed throughout our lives. It isn't necessarily taught in design school.

Suggested Solution

Changes will be needed in both undergraduate and graduate programs for interior designers. The goal is to provide the best training for interior designers at all levels of experience. The study of business practices is the basis for design communication. To ensure that student designers have skills that make it practical and economical for practicing professionals to take them into their studios, basic business practices must be a major part of every interior design curriculum. **Business practices should not be simply a course or two tacked onto a program, but the core of any design education.**

In addition, a student should have some advanced or specialized training, in CAD or the various codes, for instance. Because the working system is changing from a hierarchy to teamwork, design students should graduate from a program and be able to contribute specific skills to the firm.

A New Relationship Between Designer and Design School

I envision the relationship between design school and design student as one that lasts as long as the individual's career. The school writes a maintenance contract with graduates, agreeing to provide coaching and informational support at appropriate complexity levels. The school knows what courses the individual has completed and can design updated material to complement this knowledge and to challenge the designer.

There are times when a professional who has been practicing for ten or fifteen years might need a course that is taught today at the undergraduate level work, and that is fine. There might be other times where an undergraduate student, because of his or her previous background and interest, might be able to perform well in courses taught at the graduate level. This too should be available.

A college- or university-run continuing education program benefits the school by bringing in extra revenue. It benefits the field by standardizing the quality of information. The ideal school will be staffed by a mixture of pure academicians and professionals with practical experience in the field. It benefits the students because the extra funds can buy the very finest laboratories and teachers. It also benefits the students by mingling current students with working professionals. The younger students get the input from people with real-world experience. Returning designers get fresh outlooks on old problems from younger students. This inter-action also demands that teaching materials stay current. A revised continuing education program for past graduates may mean that design schools would need to hire trainers or teachers from outside the academic arena.

Some CEU programs currently offered through chapters of design organizations will transfer to university settings without change. Some university programs will also transfer to chapter set-tings without change. Others need new formats and/or presenta-tion guidelines. This may not be at all bad, but it would require some alteration of structure.

This sort of program will elevate the quality of a standard design education to far above what is currently achieved in a typi-cal university or college setting. For the students, it would be a con-stant demonstration of what the real world is. For the postgradu-ates, it keeps them in touch with changes in the field, and with the vital curiosity they had as students.

Easy-Access Education

The format of the training should be developed according to the demands of the subject and its complexity. Use the method of communication that will best present each subject. Some subjects might be dealt with in the form of a written bulletin accompanied by audio or video material. Some material may require days or weeks on campus or in laboratories.

These schools could also offer a group of consultants. In situations in which a person's faculty advisor or coach felt he or she needed individual attention, using a consultant might be suggested. For example, a designer could call a coach: "I ran into a lighting problem touched on by course X. I need some information that goes beyond the course. Which consultant from your list should I call?"

Information and the way it is taught can be customized to the way individuals learn: by seeing, by doing, or as intellectual constructs. Courses might be any combination of written material, videos, on-campus classes, and site visits. Ideally, they will create an opportunity for interaction between the most skilled practitioners and students.

None of this is really new. The National Technological University, an engineering graduate school in Colorado, has neither a campus nor a full time faculty. NTU beams video courses and training programs by satellite to a hundred thousand students at 130 corporations in the United States.

A New Relationship Between Design Industry and Design School

I foresee design schools becoming partners in design and partners in industry. For professionals to continue to earn a living in the field, they need the tools to make them proficient, expert, and current. These programs need to be coordinated with professional organizations for interior designers.

Why should designers do this? The field needs stronger, better-educated designers.

Why should design schools embark on a program that will require so many changes to the status quo? Design schools ought to produce students who perform better in the field. Schools should move with the changes in the industry. Enrollments to design schools have dropped. For educational institutions to grow, they need more students. Let us revitalize these campuses with programs that more directly relate to immediate needs.

Programs for design professionals must also be coordinated with the real needs of our clients, industry, and craftsmen. There are dozens of ways professional organizations and educational institutions can work together. Some programs might be offered at local chapter levels; others might spawn discussion groups at the chapter level. Schools can become almost test laboratories for industry.

Why not test new products on trained observers—design students and developing professionals? Today, many home furnishings products are test marketed in the field and revised in response to consumer complaint, which does nothing to elevate the reputation of the designer who specified it.

Other Programs of Study

In the absence of an institutional study program, we can learn by observing how other designers work and think, simply by reading biographies of designers and architects. I found the book *Charles Rennie Mackintosh: The Architectural Papers*, edited by Pamela Robertson, most interesting. It provided insights to how this very creative and artistic architect thought, with carefully chosen segments from his diary and personal work notes.

Another informal study opportunity is to form a Delphi group, as set out in Ronald Gross' *The Independent Scholar's Handbook*. The book is described as the indispensable guide for the stubbornly intelligent, which describes most interior designers. Many people who have not gotten degrees or been associated with universities have followed their own courses of study, often by linking with other people.

The Delphi process brings together people who are interested in studying and reviewing a given subject. As in a networking group, there is a standard format for interaction. Each group member shares and develops information. Each member may write an essay on an aspect of the topic, mailing it to all other members. Members critique and learn from each others' work.

Gross also targets mentoring programs as a way to further one's education. This book demonstrates that there are many other methods of learning within the educational process. Intellectual partnerships are as vital as ever. It is a very valuable process for both the student and the teacher.

Elevate Design Standards

The point is, it's time to elevate our own standards for design education. It should be practical, stimulating, and pave the way for a stronger interior design field. And let's do it in an efficient, cost-effective manner. My proposal is one way to make continuing education effective, usable, and accessible to people at all stages of their careers.

The university ought to be more than just a four- or five-year program and good-bye, you're on your own. It ought to be a continuing dialog for the designer, providing educational research and consulting services at a very high level and almost on a global basis.

The economics of today's business demonstrate that we're not doing a good enough job. We all have to work together—industry, education, professional designers—to redesign the field to raise the standards for living and working.

11

COMMUNICATE

THE PERSUASIVE POWER OF DESIGN

Interior designers have the power to persuade subtly, to direct human behavior. All people need to improve their lives, some more than others. We have the ability to support them in their selected goals and missions, and we should use it. Design changes lives and makes major differences.

The power of design is subtle, sometimes almost imperceptible, but it exists and has an effect. Interior designers learned this art of persuasion through experience in creating environments for people, and then observing the reactions.

We have the tools to create environments that make a difference. Years of human factors research have given us more information than most of us could use in a lifetime.

Now we must take our knowledge to an arena that is larger than those who buy design services. Our knowledge and abilities can help ease the effects of social and cultural deprivation.

No one other than a designer can tell you what a designer does. Let's change that. Let's be seen as leaders by designing a better world.

The principal goals of our profession are education and distribution. We have to learn to better educate our potential clients both on what design can to do improve their lives and on the proper use of products. To communicate well, we have to be able to see through their eyes. We have to accept their points of view without forgetting what we have learned through experience and schooling.

Personal service is just as important in the design industry as it is in banking. We also need to find the most effective ways to bring the product to the client with the appropriate support services. Distribution is now the most expensive segment of the price of the product.

PROBLEM SOLVING

Finding out exactly what a client wants is one of the greatest difficulties in communicating with clients. Even people who are customarily good communicators may find it hard to express what they want from a space and from a designer. What do they want? When does the space work? When doesn't it work? What issues relate to this space? If there is a problem, in what situations does the problem occur?

Defining problems quickly is essential, and a sense of confidence in your ability to solve problems is a definite plus. Do you have a simple process that helps you define problems? Are you able to design a process to fix the problem?

DESIGNER-CLIENT RELATIONSHIP

Today the client is a respected and valuable member of the design team. The acknowledgment that none of you has all the answers is part of the mutual respect that builds a good project, and *that* builds good relationships. Client relations is a lifetime project. You are never off-duty.

In the 1990s, successful firms are going to be very involved in their communities—by developing socially correct spaces, through charitable donations, through public education programs, and in just about any way you can imagine. Demonstrating an in-depth relationship with the community means you have a vested interest in the development and survival of that community.

Confidence in each other is the key. This is built through repeated contacts and shared experiences. Interior designers need to reinforce the designer-client relationship.

The term cooperation is going to be far more important to us than ever before. Are we willing to work together toward excellence for a project that is attractive and beneficial to all of the people involved? Are we willing to create *with* our client? Are we able to use that synergism that Buckminster Fuller talked about so that we are able to put two and two together so that it equals six?

Look at your own design practice and the friendships that have evolved. They grew because you developed mutual respect through working together, and working together develops a natural bond. There is no market development program that can substitute for shared experience.

A healthy designer-client relationship is essential to the future of the design business. When clients ask for information, make sure they get it immediately. Fax it and call to make sure they received it. Quality service is what customers want from other service industries. Ours is no different. **Our goal is quality service that is built upon relationships.**

The Right Way to Ask Questions

The relationship between designer and client has become one of coach and team member. Your communication style must reflect this.

We can learn a great deal and prevent misunderstandings by the way we ask questions. Part of developing a design project and developing the relationship between client and designer is in finding out what each person knows and does not know.

The way questions are asked matters. To get useful information, be inquisitive and challenging, and show concern for the client. Your questions should never appear to be critical.

Exchanging Information

Technology supports communication. There are times when communicating by E-mail, fax, modem, newsletters, or phone is best. Other times a personal visit is the wisest choice. The combination is important. Today interior designers bring much more information and materials via technology to clients and co-workers than ever before, for every portion of the job from selling to the last detail of the finished project.

Providing information is one of the primary functions of a designer, and today that information must be visual and fast. There are times when videos are an appropriate contact. We can provide expert information and demonstrations of the way furniture works via video, and use videos to get extra training for ourselves. Technology now gives us the opportunity to present the visual in an easily communicated style. There is a large body of support material and processes available to us today, and we must use all of it.

Having the information at the right time is more important than the format. Recently a client wanted to know the origin of a particular flower in a floral print named "Outlander." It looked like a rhododendron to me, but I wasn't sure, so we looked it up in the *Encyclopedia Britannica* in my office. We learned that it was a Mediterranean flower similar to the rhododendron. The explanation in the encyclopedia described a color similar to the one in her floral print. My client was very pleased to have a background story for a print that would go in her living room. This bit of information made the room more meaningful and more hers. It's part of the binding process, and reinforces our ability to sell.

Communication Schedule

Even with all the high-tech information swapping, the client wants a specific person or persons to whom they can relate and whom they can reach at any time. For your convenience and theirs, let them know a regular time when you will be available to return calls, such as between eight and ten in the morning. Once a week, give the client an update on everything that is happening on their job. This way they know that you are on top of everything. The regular updates also permit you to organize your material and to be professional when presenting it.

If you call and the person you want is not in, be sure to leave the date you are calling and a date and time when you can be reached. Make it easy.

Proposals and Contracts

The standard boiler plate contract is not going to work well in the near future. Clients want a contract or a proposal written just for them. We may pick and choose among standard contract paragraphs for legal protection, and combine this with language specific to the project.

Be careful not to promise more than you can do when you write your proposals and contracts. In proposals, give the clients precisely the information that they requested. Don't confuse the issue.

Charging

Professional expertise is why you are hired. Consider this when you write your charges. Some design firms can complete a project in one tenth the time it would take another firm, and more capably. I believe in value-based charging, billing for the quality of the job. Clients today are very interested in what they get for their investment.

SPEAKING

I'll pay more for a man's ability to speak than for any other quality he might possess. CHARLES SCHWAB, noted industrialist

We all try to communicate well, to speak to move people, but we have to try harder to organize the information into what the client can use and digest. Not only can we ourselves be overwhelmed by the details of our subject, we can overwhelm our clients.

You must first understand yourself, and really believe in what you are saying. If you truly believe, it invests your speech with more meaning. Beyond that, all you really have to do is work on the technique. In my opinion, there is no point in giving a speech if you don't believe in it.

It is important to have several critics at every speech you give. Provide them with an outline of your speech. Have you covered each item you intended to talk about? What can you do to improve your presentation?

Who is your audience and what is their level of understanding of your subject? What are their particular interests? Even though people may understand your subject, they might not be particularly interested in it. You must present your topic in a way that captures their attention.

Putting yourself into the speech will help your audience understand a little bit about you.

Present one basic idea. Decide on a topic and create a list of points that develop the subject.

Introductions are somewhat of a waste of time. It is fine to have something about the speaker's background in the program, but the introduction should be short and to-the-point.

Preparing a speech means rewriting it many times. To get it right, you must organize it so that it is precise and so that it covers everything you want it to cover.

You can be trained in the style of delivery, so rehearse and practice, sometimes with a critical audience.

Visual aids can help in making a point. However, when you are making a presentation in a darkened room, you lose a lot of the effects of personal interaction. Question and answer periods can be of great value, but they must be controlled. Think about what questions are likely to be asked, and prepare some answers in advance. If a person asks a question that is not really related to the subject matter, don't bore the audience with an answer. Suggest that the questioner speak with you after the presentation.

When I plan my speeches I start with a sheet of paper and list the subject of the speech, the location, the group I will be speaking to, and the length of the speech. I list the points that I believe are important to make this speech effective. I use that list of points as a guide when I write the speech.

Presentations

Presentations are like theatrical performances; they work best when they are planned and rehearsed. Write yourself a bare bones script of the topics you will talk about and the order. Do you need photography, slides, charts, or other visual aids? Put them in the script at the points where they are needed. Check to makes sure that all the equipment you need works.

People today are so used to excellent performances that we can't get away with off-the-cuff and spur-of-the-moment any more. Presentations have to be well polished and relevant. Don't get so involved in the show that the props or visual aids overwhelm your message.

Meetings

It has become a standard practice to send a meeting agenda to a client a few days or a week before the meeting, by mail or fax. The agenda answers these questions:

What do you expect to cover at the meeting?

Who will be attending?

What are their individual responsibilities?

What information should the client bring to the meeting?

What decisions should be made by the end of the meeting?

After the meeting, list the specific points or decisions that were made or covered during the meeting. Send this list to the client as a confirmation, and ask that the client add any relevant points you may have left out. Do this even if the meeting was a phone call. This documentation not only reassures the client of your professionalism, but it provides backup in the case of future misunderstandings.

INDUSTRY-WIDE COMMUNICATIONS EFFORTS

The industry as a whole recognizes the need for a better image, especially for interior designers. Organizations for professional designers have outreach programs.

ASID came out with a video and created a new brochure. The group also has a client-designer selection service, a toll free number that connects consumers and professional interior designers. In a year of operation, it logged 3,000 calls. This type of service has been done at the chapter level for years. Doing it nationally is a very good move.

Another communications bridge is a directory of specialists currently in the works at ASID. The association is working to identify the special skills of 21,000 practitioners, and is exploring new methods of education networking and information sharing among these specialists.

LISTENING

Relationships are based on communication and listening is essential. Listening, not how articulate we are or how clearly and distinctly we enunciate, is the way to good communication. In a relationship, listening to the people who are trying to communicate with us is what counts.

We all need to work on this. Sometimes I find myself too busy or too excited about something to wait for a clear explanation. Sometimes I am simply torn between too many things to be a good listener.

Many extremely successful and accomplished people who seem to have gotten most of what they want from life, or so it appears to me, are great listeners. They are the people who make you feel as if you are the only person in the world who matters, you are the only one that they care about, and you are the most important person in the world to them at the time you are speaking with them.

This is a wonderful ability, especially for design professionals. We build relationships with our clients, gain their trust and confidence. They must feel that we know that they are important.

Listening is so important a tool in building relationships that I think we—every design studio—should have someone review our listening skills. It might be on a monthly basis. Bring in a consultant. Let this person talk with you and the people on your staff, listen to your telephone conversations, and see how well you are communicating. The consultant could offer everyone suggestions for improving communication skills.

There are so many things we do every day without thinking because we are involved in our work. We can develop very bad habits that can really ruin areas of our relationships without our meaning to or wanting to.

Tips for good listening:

- Look at the person you are speaking to and be aware of body language and expressions. Maintain eye contact.

- Do you interrupt people? Do you start to talk before they have finished speaking? The other person has a special thought to share with you. Are you letting them fully express that thought on that subject?

- Do you sometimes talk about things or present things that people don't want to hear about? Designers can be so interested in a particular part of a project that they go on and on explaining all the details, while the client's interests lie in a completely different area. So consider what is important to the client before you explain details for hours.

- Some of us tend to do distracting things such as shuffling papers or moving things while other people are talking. This is very annoying, and can make the person you are talking with feel belittled.

- Dedicate your time and interest to the person on the other end of the telephone. Try not to do three or four other things at the same time, because you can miss important cues. And that is not good communication!

- Follow the conversation carefully so that you are not saying something or repeating something that someone has previously said. You can reiterate to enforce a point: "You said that you were interested in . . ., therefore, how would this work?"

- Keep your mind on the discussion. There have been moments when my mind was on a color scheme and all of a sudden I find the client is talking about another room or another detail. We're creative people; this happens sometimes. When it does, admit it. Say to the client "Excuse me, but I couldn't help but think about your question of a few minutes ago." Apologize for interrupting or being inattentive, then offer a possible solution if you have one. Making mistakes is human. Admitting mistakes actually endears you to the other person. You should have been listening, but even though you weren't, you were still thinking about their projects, their issues.

We all need to improve our listening skills. We need mentors, consultants, guides—someone to direct us in improving how well we listen. No matter how old we are, we can always do it a bit better. High tech instruments and other communication tools are valuable in building any type of quality relationship, but so is the ability to concentrate and listen to another person.

COMMUNICATION TOOLS

Technology makes communication fast and simple. We can choose to communicate by phone, pager, voice-mail, fax, E-mail, computer-to-computer, and a host of other methods. All of this has changed response time from a matter of weeks to a matter of hours. It's harder and harder to be out of touch. The communications industry says that one day we will have a personal phone number that will reach us anywhere in the world.

Cellular Phones

Mobile communication is a great convenience for anyone who must travel to see clients. I can't tell you how many times I've been lost but managed to get where I was going because of a cellular phone. I got my first car phone thirty years ago and I wouldn't want to be without one. Being able to contact my office or have them contact me has saved a lot of time and difficulty on projects. Get a hands-free setup in case you have to use it while driving.

The prices for cellular phones have come down considerably. Some of the early models cost approximately $3,000; now cellular phones can be bought for several hundred dollars or rented inexpensively. Considering the pace of change in technology, renting may be smarter than buying. What if you buy today and a more advanced model with just what you need comes out next month!

Investigate the kinds of service offered because it can vary greatly from company to company and locale to locale. In New York, the local charges can be as high as 60 cents a minute. Some companies offer voice-mail, which lets you return urgent calls. Those that are not urgent can wait until you are back at the office. This can save on phone bills.

There is also a difference in sound quality between cellular phones in cars and the portable cellular phones you carry in a pocket.

The wireless communication system didn't exist ten years ago, but soon we will all have wireless telephones. It would be wonderful to have one telephone number that would reach us no matter where we are.

Pagers

Pagers or beepers are useful alternatives to cellular phones, and much less expensive. Some pagers permit the caller to leave short messages, but most pagers simply alert the person carrying a pager to call his or her office.

Voice Recorders

Tape recorders have come a long way since the days of the bulky dictaphone machines. There are voice recorders the size of a credit card that can carry recorded messages of up to 75 seconds. They are perfect when you want to leave a note or catch that creative thought before you can forget it. Pen-sized recorders can tape and play for 20 seconds.

I carry a small tape recorder that is barely larger than the standard cassette it plays; it makes dictation on the spot easy. Dictation style is something that does need to be learned. You want to record only what you will need in your document to make it simpler for the person who transcribes the tape.

Many designers use pocket-sized recorders as an aid to memory. Another possibility is to call your own answering machine or voice mail system and leave the information you need as a message, so it is there when you get back to the office.

Pocket Accountants

Pocket accountants print checks, track your banking accounts and your credit cards, and do everything for you except sign your name. They even print out reports and do all the calculations. They are small enough to fit in your pocket.

Personal Digital Assistants and Handheld Computers

These pocket-sized personal computers vary widely in what they will do. The size of small paperback books, PDAs will send and receive messages, act as datebooks, keep mailing lists, and perform personal applications. Most accept handwritten pen input as well as keyed input.

Apple's Newton Message Pad was the first to allow users to write on the screen, but it took a month to teach it to recognize your handwriting. Still, it learns, and new functions are being added all the time. Sharp's Wizard just records the writing without translating it into computer code. PDAs range in price from $350 to $2,000. Most accept PCMCIA cards, which allow them to store data or run new applications. Handheld computers will do word processing and even spread sheets, as well as E-mail messaging and faxes, but the keyboards are tiny. Connector cables or wireless communication can transfer data to and from the PC or Macintosh in your office.

Portable Computers

Notebook and subnotebook computers let you work anywhere, any time—except on airplanes during take-offs and landings. Most portable computers have fax/modem abilities. Some are pen-based with keyboards, and some pen-based computers have no keyboards. I have a Macintosh Powerbook; it's just right for anyone who is not doing memory-intensive work. My co-author prefers the Toshiba laptop with Windows. Portable computers fit easily onto your already-crowded desk and can go with you to job sites as needed.

Most notebook computers offer standard sized keyboards, but can weigh up to 12 pounds. Subnotebooks weigh substantially less, some under 5 pounds. Monochrome computers are the least expensive. Passive color is pale and tends to disappear when viewed from the side. This is good if you don't want people to read over your shoulder. Dual scan passive has stronger color and is fine for nonpresentation use. For a laptop, the excellent color rendition of active matrix color can add $1,500 to $2,000 to the price—in effect almost doubling the price of the laptop.

Personal Computers

Personal computers can do almost anything that mainframes could years ago. Personal computers are real workhorses, making word processing and bookkeeping so easy that the size of support staffs has steadily dwindled in offices. PCs are message centers: we can send faxes, get voice-mail, do automatic dialing, even pay bills, place orders, and make reservations. Most of us still use keyboards, trackballs, and mice, but there are voice-activated systems. I'm waiting for voice-recognition computers. I don't mind correcting what's written, but I don't want to key it all in.

Prices have dropped so much that we can buy several PCs for what one used to cost. This new technology permits greater accuracy and makes changes easy—a flexibility that supports creativity. The role of the traditional secretary has become more interactive as computer hardware and software improve.

Peripherals

Anything that isn't already in your computer can be a peripheral— the printer, fax/modem, extra disk reader, and mouse, for example.

Inkjet printers offer near-perfect quality printing, but it is water soluble. Laser printers are the Cadillacs of the printers. If you need color printing or need to print building plans, special printers are called for.

Multi-media turns the computer into a sound machine. All computers have tiny speakers, but multi-media and a CD-ROM reader will let you play music on the PC. And the computer will greet you by name when you turn it on. This is not a priority for me, but people who play games on their computers say multi-media adds a lot to their enjoyment.

Scanners

Scanners allow you to enter information and graphics into the computer without keyboarding. Hand-scanners require a steady hand; electronic pasting of text is required. Optical character recognition (OCR) scanners recognize typefaces and type sizes. Without OCR, print is just a pattern of dots to the computer. OCR scanners sometimes let you record information in the format of your word processor.

If you plan to do a lot of scanning, a full-page OCR scanner will save you time. It takes several passes of a hand scanner to read in all the copy on a standard $8^{1}/_{2} \times 11$-inch page. The full-page scanner can be used to scan documents to send by internal fax boards. You cannot yet use the same scanner for DOS and Mac computers.

Local Area Networks

Local area networks (LANs) give access to the same information instantly. It's a software and hardware solution. A separate computer acts as a server; it serves up files and programs to other computers that are called clients. A dedicated server serves the network and is not a workstation besides. You need at least a 486 to act as a server. You also need software to manage the network. Novell Lite, Netware, LANtastic, and Windows for Workgroups are some of the programs. The cost is about $200 per station. If your firm is spread out, it might make sense to build a LAN.

Laptops with PCMCIA II slots can be easily attached to a network. Another solution is to get an adapter that plugs into the parallel printer port. Some notebooks have docking stations. Others operate by radio waves.

CD-ROM Drives

CD-ROM disks store up to 650 megabytes of information—or an encyclopedia—on a single disk platter. These disks are great for references such as zip codes, data from encyclopedia, legal and medical references, and databases.

CD-ROM readers now come in three different speeds: single speed is considered slow, double speed is the norm, and triple speed is devoutly to be wished for. The CD-ROM reader must be matched to the type of computer you own, DOS/Windows or Mac. However, you can play music disks on either.

Bulletin Board Systems

Bulletin Board Systems, or BBSs, are a major lifeline in the information age. BBSs are interactive networks for information and ideas that are accessible to almost anyone with computer equipment and a modem. More than 14 million people use bulletin boards in some form today, for information, research, investment services, playing games, and just chatting. There are many local BBSs affiliated with user groups.

Bulletin-boarding has become a kind of culture, a communal meeting place. Howard Rheingold (*The Virtual Community*) writes that the BBS society "feels more like a ... gift economy where people do things for one another out of a spirit of building something between them."

Online systems include America On-Line, Prodigy Computer Service, Dow Jones Retrieval, and the Internet, to name a few. There is a monthly charge for service. The Internet alone is used by over 20 million individuals and organizations around the world. It carries more information than any other format, such as newspapers, televisions, and telephones. Seminars on how to get on line with the Internet are sell-outs at conventions.

Future applications for the interior design field include interacting with our resources to send and receive with up-to-date information, such as research done in factories and testing centers. This service could advise us of projects around the world and applications of certain types of products to specific situations. Information that once came to us via catalog once or twice a year could be updated at a second's notice.

It is also a way to ease the isolation of working alone. Information exchanges via E-mail and modem could improve our working relationships and even act as a spur to creativity, especially now that the graphic interfaces have improved.

There are BBS addresses for all sorts of special interest groups on topics ranging from soap operas to environmental activism. The Internet yellow pages had a listing for architecture but none for interior design. As of June 1994, ASID did not have a BBS where interior designers could exchange information.

I think the BBS would be a great place to share information. It's one way design schools could update their graduates. We could even get access to design-related research.

Databases

Any article, book, or government document published within the last four years can probably be retrieved through on-line databases. Libraries carry the more widely used databases. Dialog

Information Services, a pioneer among on-line databases, owns databases such as Lexis, a legal database; Dun and Bradstreet, financial information on businesses; Business Index, a business database; ABI/Inform, index and abstracts of 850 business and trade journals; and Infotrak, an index of popular magazines such as *The Wall Street Journal*.

Technical Advances for the Near Future

AT&T is expected to announce an alliance with Silicon Graphics to bring about the interactive services that will let customers send and receive video over AT&T phone lines. Silicon Graphics video servers can store the large amounts of information needed to operate an interactive video service.

The latest trend in computing is social computing, a convergence of computer networks, telephone services, groupware, handheld electronic devices, cable television, and the Internet and other on-line services, mixed in with the entertainment industry, traditional news media, and other communications technologies.

The rise of social computing will shift the emphasis of computing devices away from simple number crunching and data base management to wider ranging forms of business communication. Computing power will move into the pockets of the worker.

HOW DO YOU FIND THE RIGHT COMPUTER SYSTEM?

There are still no easy answers in choosing computers. In the early 1990s, many firms used DOS-based computers for their word-processing and Mac-based computers for graphic work. Connective cables allowed information swaps. Both operating systems allow the option of larger computer screens. Anything other than standard is still expensive. Microsoft's Windows application has made the differences between the two systems much smaller. And Apple (Mac) offers dual systems in the same computer, which makes information exchange very simple.

The basic computer setup for either operating system includes computer with monitor, keyboard, and mouse or trackball; a printer; fax/modem; and CD-ROM reader. Get as much memory as you can afford, and try to buy an upgradeable system. Most designers need a word processing program, a database manager, and a graphics program. You'll have to decide whether to network with other designers in your firm or run independently.

Experts advise you to find your software first and then to buy the computer you need to run it on. If the software calls for x amount of RAM (active memory, as opposed to storage memory), you need at least that much or the program will either run slowly or freeze up the computer. Expect to spend $1,000 to $5,000 on software.

Decide whether the standard monitor is large enough, or whether you will need a 17- or 21-inch monitor. The 21-inch monitor is recommended for presentation work.

The standard 486 with eight megabytes of RAM (Random Access Memory) is at an all-time price low, under $2,000. Macs are also at an all-time price low. Buy from a reputable dealer, and expect someone from the company to install the software and to train you and your staff. Although other employees may understand the programs better, they won't always be there to help you. Learn to use the computer yourself.

Right now, buying a computer and the software is labor-intensive. It's still a matter of researching what is available and then physically testing the computers to develop a preference.

You no longer have to be a computer programmer, engineer, or technophile to set up the computer. The computer industry standard is now what they call plug and play. You take the boxes home, hook up the cables, and turn on the machine. Then you spend a couple of hours loading it with the appropriate software, although a lot of computer manufacturers are shipping computers with software preloaded.

If you are buying your first computers or are unhappy with your current system, talk with other design firms. See what they have, what they like, and why they like it. Go to computer stores and look at computers. Personal preference is the best indicator.

Test the keyboard. Do you have to pound the keys or are they a pleasure to use? Does the mouse fit your hand? Is it immediately responsive?

If you already have a computer and want to add peripherals such as multimedia or CD-ROM readers, read the backs of the boxes. The manufacturers will tell you which makes and models of computers are most compatible with their products.

In some industries, professional organizations have polled their membership on the types of computers and programs they were using, and published the results with recommendations and reasons why. I asked my accountant for the accounting industry guide to computers. Some industries have developed proprietary software applications that demand a certain computer operating system. A specification program for use with WordPerfect and DOS-based computers was developed with the AIA. All of this helps narrow your selection.

You may want to hire a consultant to find the computer and software mix that is best for your firm. Some consulting firms will customize the applications as well as recommending computers, peripherals and software. Some software firms include training with the software package.

No matter what, learn to use the computer. It's a timesaver with a memory that can hold more than yours can. And so many communications devices interface with computers that they are hard to ignore.

12

THE DESIGN TEAM

People and knowledge are a firm's greatest assets.

You are often closer to the people you work with than to family, friends, or neighbors because you spend much more time with them. They share some of their great passions during working hours. During personal tragedies, the people at work are the ones who become part of the support system.

To look at our work group as anything other than an extended family is a mistake. This should be considered when selecting where we want to work, who to employ, and which independent contractors will be part of our design team.

In the design company of tomorrow, *people* are very important, both the staff and the clients. Every member of our design team, from clients and staff to craftspeople and suppliers, must feel important to the project, and empowered and rewarded by their experience.

Every project is an opportunity to learn and develop our individual abilities. Knowledge is important, and we should always be ready to master additional information. Making mistakes is part of mastery.

The design firm of today must be structured to get a job done, and the work process must develop each staff person's talents as well as developing a coalition of the client and the design team. That is the vision and the mission for today's design firm.

This isn't happening in the distant future. It is happening now. What impresses today is action.

Technology is erasing many of the boundaries of the past. We now have opportunities to interact, communicate, and perform more quickly and accurately than ever. We are working at much higher levels of complexity. We have had to become smarter and more independent. Because decisions are being made at all levels, everyone in the company must be well-informed and qualified to make a decision. The demand for quick decisions means you can no longer afford to go back to the office for the project leader's decision—something you had to do before, because there was only one person with all the information. Today information is available to everyone on the team at the same time.

There will be greater flexibility in our workstyle so that it fits our personal styles. This brings us flexible hours, flexible locations and compensation by the project. No matter what else changes, we still have to get the job done. The key to business today is the ability to deal with things quickly, using the talents, abilities, excitement and energy of all of the people who work with us. The ability to move quickly is important. It's not the time for large companies with heavy overheads. It is the time for groups with the ability to move quickly and intelligently.

ORGANIZATIONAL CHARTS

The organizational chart in design firms probably should be thrown away, or at least redesigned. The self-managing work team should become the basic organizational building block, according to Tom Peters in his book *Thriving on Chaos*.

Status is not part of a good design practice. Today, the trend is toward a flatter organization that groups people in multi-disciplinary teams to achieve a customer-driven operation. In the near future, we are going to be working with our clients to build excellent projects.

Design is much more of a team effort, which means that we have to really learn to interact and to relate in a very different way than we have done. The ability to change from methods based on competition to working as members of a team may determine whether we survive.

We have to stop thinking about our own preferences and start thinking about the client's problem and how we can solve it. The members of a design team need to understand that they are working *with* the client; that the client is the key to the design process. This provides direction and makes work less repetitious. Someone has to take the responsibility for the project, and usually the team organizer serves as the leader or facilitator. The team itself may select a leader, or allow leadership to pass to anyone who is familiar with the subject matter and the purpose. Leadership also can come from the person whose issue needs to be explored.

Design teams are lead by a vision shared by all of it members. Some new systems of business management take on this model— which is based on the traditional approach of design teams: define the problem and build a team of the best people to solve it.

DEFINING THE TEAM

Teamwork isn't attending meetings and taking notes; it involves a common purpose, a sense of interdependence, and shared accountability.

The interdisciplinary nature of design projects means you will be building and rebuilding new teams for almost every project. The core of your team, designers and support staff, may stay the same, whereas contractors, vendors, and clients vary.

In building a team of people to work together on design projects, research and experience will show you how the pieces fit together. You can't arbitrarily throw people and vendors together and have it magically work. Sometimes it will, but just as often these unplanned partnerships fail because the team members don't have the interpersonal skills to make effective team members.

There is normal resistance to this concept, mostly from people who have learned to operate within a traditional organization. A few normal worries include concern over loss of control by managers, the burden of learning new skills, fewer opportunities to gain titled positions, and possible loss of compensation and reward for individual performance.

Complementary skills are important, but each team member should acquire the ability to look at things from more than one point of view. As the team evolves, it will develop its own standards of measurement and acceptable behavior. Success or failure is becoming the joint responsibility of an intelligence-based staff.

At first, the team organizer leads the way in defining the team's purpose, goals, and objectives.

The company may be called a design community because everyone who is there wants to work together. It is not necessarily a group without leaders. There is probably more than one leader. An ideal team is made up of people with different capabilities who work toward the same goal, contributing their talents when they are needed. This is an environment in which it is safe to demonstrate abilities and practice skills. Sometimes we will make mistakes, but the design community environment allows us to take chances, to learn from our mistakes, and to grow. This type of organization builds an experienced team.

Although design firms grow by expanding the disciplines they offer, you don't necessarily have to be the sole employer of everyone on your team. You may have to offer specialties in-house because they are not available in your geographic area. On the other hand, having an in-house specialist may damage your relationships with other consultants.

Vendors and craftspeople are also members of the team, sharing the desire to complete projects efficiently and with a high level of quality. We cannot afford to put our vendors and craftspeople in an antagonistic position. If we are going to achieve our goals in this competitive market, the vendors and crafts people we work with have to be part of our company, bound by a marriage of respect and understanding.

In the past, adversarial relationships with vendors were accepted. The system encouraged it. Today we cannot accomplish much without teamwork. We will have fewer resources but they will be much more important to us. **Everything is based on relationships and relationships with deep substance**.

A community or a company is a process, not a building or a

location. Your company may have many types of organizational structures, but it must be made up of people who are involved and are committed to the process of mastering a given subject for a particular goal. Success or failure in building the company team depends in part on the ability of the players to communicate. During the changeover, there may be many periods of confusion or chaos, but it is a necessary trial and error process. The more we work together, the better we get at it.

LEADERSHIP

The goal of management is not to empower subordinates but to liberate them. OREN HARRARI

At first I didn't agree with Oren Harrari, who is a professor at the University of San Francisco and a speaker with the Tom Peters group. After I thought about it I began to see that it is true, especially for the interior design discipline.

Designers want freedom. We want the excitement that comes from developing our talents, and we need the freedom to do it any way we want, not as someone else thinks it should be done. If we really want our teammates to use their talents, we have to give them opportunities to develop those talents. Of course we want a favorable outcome for our efforts, but developing leaders means allowing our team members to learn from their own mistakes.

Liberation grows out of self confidence. Knowing what we are good and bad at lets us relate better to the people on our teams. We really can't be good leaders without confidence in ourselves.

Arthur Ashe said that each time he went out to play tennis, he would try to do one or two things better than he had done before. He never tried for a 100 percent improvement, he just tried to be a little better. A steady three percent improvement over time made Ashe a top tennis player. I think good leaders also try to top themselves every day.

To lead people, we really have to listen to them and to respect their opinions. One reason the *I-Power* program is so good is that it is directed at coordinating efforts of the whole team, getting ideas from everyone.

Enthusiasm is important. I don't want to follow someone who is not enthusiastic and is not exciting, someone who pounces on my mistakes in public and praises me in private. An enthusiastic leader looks for the opportunity to compliment, develop, and encourage other people. An effective leader can sell anyone or anybody on an idea or a product.

Many successful people say that they are careful not to expose themselves to negative people. And I think this is extremely important. We need to surround ourselves with people who add to our abilities, whose attitudes nurture us. This is a hard one to achieve, but it's worth working on.

I-Power

I-Power is a management concept that involves asking everyone in the company to come up with ideas to improve the company. The focus is on gathering small ideas and giving immediate response. The goal is a free and easy exchange of views. The company benefits in two ways: by the ideas and by the team spirit this approach fosters.

The I-Power program puts the power to change in the hands of people with practical experience. In the beginning, workers are often skeptical, thinking this is just another words-rather-than-action program. But there are small rewards distributed monthly for ideas that are accepted and used. The monthly awards publicize the program, ideas and accomplishments. I-Power gets people involved in the team process by making testing ideas a standard practice. People like putting their own ideas into action, more so than things imposed by a hierarchical process.

In larger companies, each person is given I-power pads. I-Power suggestion boxes are placed where they cannot be missed. To get the ball rolling, the leader may suggest areas that need improvement. Employees have access to a selection of publications and videos to use as reference materials, so when they know something is wrong but don't have an answer yet, they aren't limited by their own experience.

Elements of the program will adapt easily into the workstyles of most interior designers, as it is very like the studio system of learning. It is normal for us to discuss a problem with everyone in the firm, and then to ask for ideas. The people who are most familiar with a particular process often have ideas on how to streamline it. I like I-Power. It promotes individual responsibility. If I am away from my desk and a member of my staff knows the answer to a client's question, the client does not have to wait until I return.

This process was developed by Martin Edelston, president of *Boardroom Reports*. He uses it in his own company with great success and has written a book about it. An I-Power training course is available throughout the country and a newsletter reports on doings of I-Power seminar alumni.

Taking the Lead

Leadership is much more an art, a belief, a condition of the heart, than a set of things to do. The visible signs of artful leadership are represented ultimately in its practice. MAX DEPREE

In real life, someone has to take the responsibility for leadership. Not everyone in the group is going to be interested in, or capable of, creating new opportunities for business. Someone must take the lead. Most people prefer a stable working environment; changes make them unhappy. We also know that most people don't have the interpersonal skills to be leaders.

It usually takes a strong person to lead a group in forming a communal design firm. After it is created, its many leaders share the burdens and rewards of leadership. In the end, the initiator-leader works much more as facilitator or a coach than as a dictator.

People want four things from their leaders: direction, meaning, hope and results, according to the Peter F. Drucker Foundation for Non-Profit Management.

An organization based on teamwork must have a philosophy, a set of values from which it operates. Developing a direction and inspiring others to work with you in achieving it are important to your organization. This must happen at every level. It is the responsibility of each of us to make this change.

Four main elements are part of the successfully decentralized company:

1. Shared responsibility within an organization works best when the objective is worthwhile. It should meet the individual needs, values, and goals of the different members of the group. Each of us must see and believe that our work is worth doing, creating, and devoting our lives to accomplishing.

2. Each of us must be committed to the same goal. It has to be easy, simple, and clear.

3. We must communicate it. We must be able to get other people to invest in this shared vision.

4. We must encourage and reinforce our efforts because progress is never a straight line. Progress needs constant reminders and reinforcements.

As designers, we have all worked on projects where the client says "I did it myself." We have to learn to take this as a compliment. Lao-tzu, in the *Tao Te Ching*, wrote, "True leaders inspire others to do great things and, when the work is done, their people proudly say, 'we did this ourselves'." Designers are called into leadership roles in many different ways, but we direct, encourage, and lead people to perform and do things far beyond what they would have done without us. We create the shared vision and often assist with that process, so designer is synonymous with leader.

We also have to learn to be followers, to take the directions our clients give us, and to understand the opportunities and limitations of our crafts and of nature. It is our job, however, to take on the responsibility of leadership. I think we have now learned to follow only someone whose value patterns and philosophies are similar to our own. Follow someone you can respect.

Leaders are people who do the right things. Managers are people who do things the right way. Peter Drucker says leadership is a matter of how to be and not how to do. He says it is ethics full time, value focused.

A great leader doesn't waste other people's time, whether it is staff or clients. The vision must be projected clearly enough to direct people effectively. Leaders must take the time to clarify what they want done. Define your own personal objectives and mission first. You can't possibly share something you haven't thought out clearly.

It's a step in the right direction to define the problems. When the problems are defined, you have the key to what your firm can do to handle these problems successfully.

When you don't get an appropriate response to a request, find another way to phrase it or another way to get something done. There is no point in blaming other people. Either you did not present your request properly or the structure doesn't exist for you to receive the appropriate response.

Getting the best from people means defining the specific results you want. Everyone must share your concept of success. It isn't enough to say, "Do the best you can." That is abstract and too hard to interpret.

Reinforce good performance by letting people know you really appreciate their efforts. Positive reinforcement can be worth more than any other kind of interaction.

Shall I Lead?

A leader doesn't have to be the chief executive officer of the company, but each group needs someone with the power and ability to make things happen. A leader can develop from almost any part of the company.

The team concept of doing business and the servant-leader concept are similar. Max DePree said, "The first responsibility of a leader is to define reality. The last is to say thank you. In between, the leader must become a servant and a debtor. That sums up the progress of an artful leader."

The leader's job is to keep everyone's attention on the process.

Leaders must be visionaries; they set goals; they are in front, moving, sharing, dreaming, and creating that mission. This is the reason why they exist.

Leaders often come from very different backgrounds. They don't necessarily decide that they are going to be leaders, but they develop into leadership roles because they see a need and a way to accomplish it. Sometimes leadership is just a natural process.

Leadership training is beneficial. We can learn to be leaders by recognizing our strengths and developing techniques that will help us in our leadership methods.

CONSULTANTS ON CALL

In this action-oriented, information-based era, teams form and re-form constantly. We will be blending the cultures of our clients, the design world (not just interior design, but all the other design disciplines), our crafts, and our resources.

For a team to work efficiently, there must be a rapport and a mutual respect among its members. In the extended team of designer, craftspeople, and vendors, everyone stands up for his or her own industry, and they are right to do it. But somebody's going to have to make a judgment call because on a project there are limits. We have so much money. We have so much space. We have so much whatever. Who determines what is the best "buy" for the client in a given situation?

Well, the interior designer makes that decision, but with the help of consultants they have learned to know and to trust. I don't want to make that decision based on information from somebody who is new to my group. I want to see other projects by this potential teammate. I want to know who's worked with them. I want indicators that allow me to judge how much I can rely on this person's information.

Your search may begin with a directory of consultants, but you should look at their references, including a list of projects they've worked on and with which firms. Unfortunately, learning new things takes time, and it does get expensive. When I take a project, I try to anticipate what the snags will be, how much of the project demands that I learn something new, and I use Pareto's 80/20 ratio—only 20 percent of the project should be a totally new experience for us.

The same ratio applies to consultants. Eighty percent of your consultants should be people and firms you have worked with before; you know them, you know which issues to trust their judgment on and what their exaggerated issues are. Sometimes people overplay or underplay certain things. When you know the kind of response to expect, working together is easier.

The new person brought into the team is your 20 percent; the rest of the team is your 80 percent. You can then make an accurate assessment of how much of that opinion to incorporate into your design.

Groups That Can Refer You to Accredited Consultants

Academy of Professional Consultants and Advisors
123 NW Second Ave.
Portland, OR 97209; 503-222-8834

American Consultants League
1290 Palm Ave.
Sarasota, FL 34235; 813-952-9290

Council for Consulting Organizations
230 Park Ave.
New York, NY 10169; 212-697-9693

National Bureau of Professional Management Consultants
3577 Fourth Ave.
San Diego, CA 92103; 619-297-2210

National Consultant Referrals Inc.
8445 Camino Santa Fe, Suite 207
San Diego, CA 92121; 619-552-0111

WHAT MAKES A GOOD TEAM MEMBER?

If you like a person, chances are your client will like that person too. If something about that person makes you uncomfortable, your client will probably feel the same way. In building your team, think about what makes a good team member.

How well do they express themselves? The people who work with you should have good communication skills. Do they appear enthusiastic and encouraging? Do they relate to you in a way that you would like to see them relate to your clients? Are they able to explain design in terms the client will understand? Look at this, as well as their work and education experience, before you consider adding this person or that contractor to your team.

I've heard it said that the collective IQ of a team is half that of the least intelligent team member. It's something to consider when forming your team.

Sometimes the person whose skills and willingness to share knowledge, to challenge and develop you is not right for the time or the project. I think we do need challenge, but let's be careful who we select to challenge us.

Some people will say they can do something that they have no experience with and can't really do. As head of the firm or team leader, we are responsible for reviewing their abilities and determining just what they can really do. Resumes and portfolios can be deceptive. While you may be familiar with the name of the design school or the project, how do you know the precise curriculum or the scope of the applicant's responsibilities?

Rather than be surprised on your project, talk with their former employers before any hiring decision is made. This does require written permission. Ask the applicant for the name of the person at their previous job(s) who really knows them best and if it is all right to talk to that person. Does their present employer know that he or she is looking for another position?

For both prospective employees and contractors, get as much information as you can. Visit the project; don't just look at a photograph. The site will give you plenty of clues. Find out what kind of clients they've been working with. Find a way to speak to some of their clients and learn what the clients think of them.

To protect your company, you must have appropriate permission forms signed. Some sample forms are in my book *The Interior Design Business Handbook*.

Tom Peters says that the next time a job candidate dozes off during the interview, wake him up and hire him. It was you who put him to sleep. The point is that we need people who are excited by life, who design for the new world, who use their imaginations to develop a new world, rather than simply trying to please the market.

Every Team Member Must Be a Business Person

Everyone in your firm must understand what it takes to make the business work and what it takes to service that client. They need to know precisely what services you offer are and exactly what it means to run the firm in a profitable way. By profitable I mean not just financially, but in terms of exposure to different kinds of work, in staff development opportunities, and in gaining entrée to another field.

Today every member of a team must know something about the next person's job. It isn't like it used to be when one person ran the accounts, someone else did the selling, and another person did the designing.

Everyone ought to have some understanding of general business communication skills before they leave college. At a minimum, we should know what makes that good communication base and what makes a company profitable. Communicating is part of relationships, and good designer-client relationships make a company profitable.

All designers and support staff must be sales oriented. We can no longer afford to have people who are not client conscious. If you don't have the desire or the social skills to deal with these relationships, you're going to have a very difficult time getting a job in this next decade.

All successful firms need to have an in-depth relationship with the community. Marketing and selling on its own is not enough.

Internships

Under the Fair Labor Standard, any firm that uses student interns must meet certain conditions. A student cannot replace a regular employee and is not guaranteed a job at the end of his or her internship. Both the company and the intern are aware that the intern is not entitled to income during the internship. However, you may choose to pay them a lump sum to be applied toward education. The intern must receive some training from your company, and this training should be comparable to what he or she would receive at a vocational school. Most importantly, the training of the intern is the primary goal—not necessarily having them work for your company. The student intern must learn procedural skills.

Rainmakers

The interior design and furnishings field has not trained, developed, or created many rainmakers. And what we need are rainmakers. We need people who create the project, not just sell or respond to a need but often create the need or the desire. We have people who know how to make a project happen, but few who know where to go to drum up a need for our services, convince the client that our firm is the best for the job, and bring the project home so the rest of the firm has work.

Independent Contractors

An independent contractor doesn't have a grand title, doesn't have a position, and isn't assured an income—he or she does what it takes to get the job done and then gets paid for that given job. We interior designers have been doing this throughout our careers. We don't really have the security in our jobs that other professionals may have. We don't have tenure, a guaranteed salary or a retirement plan. But we are used to doing a project and completing it.

When you join a firm, you are not just filling a prescribed position, you are creating your own position. You are bringing in talents and abilities that would not be there otherwise. We need to think of ourselves as people who create and design jobs, not as people who are given jobs.

Today, many people are not directly employed, but work on an assignment basis or as independent contractors. This is happening in the corporate world and the design field is not far behind.

If you are an independent designer who leads a design firm, it is essential to have independent contractor forms signed by anyone who is working with your firm, to define the work to be done, who is responsible for what, and the method of compensation.

This brings up the question of employment structures and taxes. Independent contractors normally carry their own insurance and pay their own taxes. The Internal Revenue Service will often question firms on this basis because they would much prefer seeing many of these contractors listed as employees. So it is important to have up-to-date documentation. The IRS believes that a person who earns his entire income for the year from your firm is an employee. Unless it is clear that the person works for other firms and not just your own, there could be problems.

HANDLING ORGANIZATIONAL CONFLICTS

When groups start to move, this automatically destroys some of the organizational structure. In many cases the structure has taken years to build. How do you ease the transition? If you simply add another person, you create feelings of job insecurity among the existing staff, and they may resist necessary changes. But if you set a time limit on the relationship and make it clear that the new person is there only to help manage the transition, you make it easier for the staff to accept suggestions. Easier in fact than if you, the CEO, made the suggestions.

A firm nearby recently combined two offices that were only five miles apart. There was no reason their clients could not drive that extra five miles. Combining the facilities freed money to use on additional equipment. Integrating the staff simplified communications. Logistically and financially, joining the two offices made sense.

But the offices had been run as two completely isolated structures. Anticipating clashes in management styles, one of the senior partners decided that they needed a professional manager. The existing management had run the organization for years and had done so reasonably well. They had personal relationships with the senior partners. When a new management person was brought in at a level above the existing management, they were cut out of the loop and resented it. Bringing in another boss who is being paid two or three times what the rest of the staff makes may only cause a firm to fall apart. I've seen this happen many times.

Combining staffs is very difficult to do without preparation. It probably would have worked better had they brought in a consultant to help them reorganize, adjust, and improve their efficiency—an interim person rather than a permanent new boss. Some firms even bring in transition teams. With a time limit and the understanding that the person is there as a trainer, you can avoid unrest and the feeling that the new person will jeopardize their positions.

For example, to resolve a conflict situation, some churches will not permit the parish to take on a new pastor. They hire an interim pastor to work with the church for one or two years, and work out the problems. Then they bring in the permanent person.

Change increases the pressures on everyone in the office. CEOs and senior staff worry where the income is coming from and are very aware of how much work they must produce to generate that income. They juggle legal issues, government labor regulations, and myriad other everyday pressures. Employees fear for their jobs. Everyone is under pressure, and if we don't protect both the staff and the professionals by removing some of the pressures and putting back the pleasures, the whole work process will suffer.

With any change in a management system, there are, inevitably, some people who will no longer fit in as well. Even if you have precisely the right staff for team management, transition can be rough. In this situation a consultant-trainer could help these people see new opportunities and their abilities to contribute. It is a major adjustment, both for the staff and for the leader.

Teamwork means empowering the employees to make decisions and act on them. Sometimes they will make the wrong decision, but how else will they learn and acquire the experience that leads to making right decisions?

I see a dire need for a specialist in management therapy. The point is to look at change or issues of conflict as problems that need resolution. Company therapists—consultants who scrutinize organizations and suggest what can be done to accustom the existing staff to a new work style and new demands—can help solve problems. In the top-down style of management, you could say, "This person is out and that person is in." But unless the person is actively destructive, why would you do that? If the person has been working with you for 10 years or longer, he or she has valuable knowledge of the way your firm works and could help ease the transition once he or she is reoriented. Of course they're going to have be converted to the new way of thinking, and you may not be the person to do it. Sometimes that conversion is handled more effectively by someone outside the firm.

Bond the Branches of the Design Industry

The branches of the design industry should form closer bonds so that:

- We understand each other's practices;
- We can better use each other's products;
- We can produce a higher quality of work;
- We can make better use of time, energy and money;
- We can stimulate each other;
- We can close the information gap between manufacturer and consumer, and manufacturers know they are producing what the consumer wants;
- We can all learn from each other;
- We can prevent mistakes;
- We can surpass what we are individually capable of;
- We can create a product whose value is immediately apparent to everyone;
- We can find a way to bring the benefits of design to all income levels.

13

DIRECTIONS

INDUSTRY AS PARTNER

I've written elsewhere that the uneasy relationship between designers and their resources, which used to be an accepted part of doing business in the design community, is no longer acceptable. One reason is that we simply cannot afford it. We need each other too much.

Today most firms will be doing more work with fewer staff members. Fees are much smaller, the volume of space per square footage will be up, and you will be doing more work with less time and less money. This is not unique to the design field; it's business today. With better-educated clients and heavier responsibilities for design firms, we need stronger and better ties to our resources.

Teamwork, working as part of a team made up of marketing people, engineers, order clerks, and installers, can strengthen the interior design profession. People on the same team share information, and collaboration speeds the process.

You can only design from what you know. If you don't know about materials or products, you can't incorporate them in your design. Our projects demand specific information, yet too narrow a focus can hurt the quality of your design. Exploring and investigating new products and materials are basic parts of design.

There is a tremendous amount of research involved in any project. There is a demand for much more detailed specifications and reasons to use or select a specific product.

Our resources can be part of our search committees, alerting us to newly available products and vendors we may not previously have worked with. Their experience with the way products are used can help determine the feasibility for a given project, in terms of cost and performance level.

Our resources can supply all types of code information and create a context that helps us judge where their products fit this project. They also have approvals and documentation on file. These can be faxed or sent to us by modem. This saves time.

Our resources can review their product lines to let us know exactly what will work in a specific situation, if a product is difficult to install, and whether we have chosen the right products. Their experience on a range of projects may lead them to suggest possible product modifications or other products in their lines.

Our resources can easily furnish the information on samples, technical data, information, specifications, and details. They probably know from experience how their products can be combined with other products, and may have suggestions of which other products relate. They know their competition; they probably also know of product lines that work well with theirs.

Our resources can provide budget information as we develop a project, so that we can determine the budget before the project is complete. Design resources need to find ways to update information to designers continually. E-mail, information transfers by modem, diskettes, and faxes make immediate updates possible. And with the swift changes that take place today, we are going to need instant information updates from our resources.

The Difference in Cost and Quality

We need to understand in detail why one piece of furniture costs $12,000 when a similar piece costs only $2,000. We need to be able to give the client well-informed reasons for the difference in cost and quality of the pieces we present. I believe that the clients of today want things that are fine and unusual, and of higher quality.

Education bonds a client to the designer. They come to us for resource information; we ought to know enough to be able to explain the reality and the romance of decorative art products. We need to be able to interpret solutions on our own, rather than having to rely on the assistance of manufacturer's representatives.

Carnegie Fabrics has begun to sponsor week-long study trips for designers, to learn the story of fabric production in detail. This is a fine example of the kind of sharing that ought to go on within the home furnishings and design industry.

In exchange, designers should make every effort to inform resources of the exact demands being placed on their product in a specific installation. We should tell manufacturer's representatives how their products work in our projects, especially when they work well. When a minor modification will update a product or make it more usable, pass the information along.

When industry resources complain that interior designers have no soul, that we are only going through the mechanics of design, we should take notice, because we are sending the wrong signals. Any time a resource brings a problem to your attention, ask for specifics. Is it just you, or is it all designers? Is this a recent development or has it been going on for awhile? What does this person think you should do about the problem?

We should happily do anything we can to improve the flow of information in and among our industry.

FUTURE WORK STYLES

Skill Ratings

For each project we do, we often form new teams of carpenters, cabinetmakers, plumbers, electricians, marble workers, and other craftspeople. A system of qualification and rating of skill levels could make hiring unknown craftsmen less of a gamble. This could work not just for the crafts, but for entire companies. We might hire a company, but individual skill ratings would allow us to know how qualified its workers were to deal with our particular project. Today on design projects we use union or nonunion workers.

What I would like to see is a system very like the traditional guild system of medieval Europe, with apprentice, journeyman, and master craftsman skill levels. In a guild system, members are defined by their abilities. When you hired a Level 1 or a Level 6 person, you would know that they were capable of doing that level of work. This would be good for both those doing the hiring and the craftsmen. Craftsmen would be automatically qualified according to their skill levels. They could move around the country, from project to project, without losing their positioning.

The guild or union would be responsible for devising the requirements for a training program as well as the grading or rating system. Craftsmen could be ranked by a system that involved recommendations of master craftsmen and actual work experience.

When you do a wide variety of work then the guild system is needed; if you are a specialist and offer turnkey service, your craftspeople may work only for you, or be under a single company structure.

What if there were an internal rating system of skill levels for designers and the allied crafts?

A designer who excels at simply specifying fabrics and furniture placement has skills that are different from a designer who develops the interior space requirements for amounts and types of space and their relationships to each other.

Right now, some designers are affiliated with a professional organization and some are not. There is no way for us to know, and no way for the public to know, what skill level we have achieved. There is no way to know at a glance which designers to add to our teams for specific projects.

There is a need for designers at all levels, from the much maligned decorator whose real skill is in color, fabric, and inventive uses of fabric, to designers capable of planning building requirements and specifying corporate campuses for the largest Fortune 500 firms. There are many levels in between.

There is an informal rating system at the larger design firms, with project designer and design assistant. A more formal skill rating system can only help the industry. Because companies are so flexible, we need to know that Designer A can handle construction management and Designer B is excellent in the planning stages for giant projects, but is fully qualified to handle whatever is necessary in residential work and commercial design projects up to a certain level of complexity.

Giving the public a single meaning for the word "designer" creates an identity. But within that umbrella term there are many types of designers. We don't all have the same aptitudes. There are designers who are better at finish work or dressing a room than at construction detailing. Rather than insist that all of us perform at exactly the same level, like machinery, let's be realistic and recognize our differences.

Interior Designers Could Use Agents

The acting profession has agents; why not interior design? I think the agent system—where the agents know the strengths of a designer and find her or him appropriate work—would be excellent for interior designers. Karen Fisher's Designer Previews, Charlotte Peters Inc., and Designer Referral of NY are designer referral agencies. They present designer's portfolios to potential clients, finding and making matches.

Just as designers have had to expand and change their services, I think referral agencies may grow and change into full-service agents. Some may offer career advice, suggesting that designers pursue specific types of projects, or that they get additional training, or that they pair up with another specialist. For example, an agent may tell a designer, "This is your strong spot, this is the way I see business going, and these are the places that I see you fitting in best; therefore let's go after this type of job."

I see agents as having the skills to look at your educational background and opportunities, get to know you as a person and then be able to guide you as a mentor, coach, or career developer. It may not be done by a single person, but by a group of people within the agency. One person might provide the educational direction, a second might make matches with other specialists, and a third may provide sales and marketing presentation.

Interior designers love to design. Most of us don't want to interrupt our directed creative efforts searching for the right kind of client. Once the potential clients have been screened, we are willing to learn the material, rehearse, make a great presentation, and really study the job. But some of that screening could be done better, perhaps, by specialists.

There are employment agencies, headhunters such as The Viscusi Group, that dealt in career-long positions a few years ago. Now their placements tend to be for the term of the project. There has been change in the way designers are employed and in the way design employment agencies operate. So my vision of the future is not all that far out. A full-service design employment/placement agency that provides career strategy and market placement advice and suggests profitable teams would have a niche.

Very often it helps to have someone outside your firm review your goals, objectives, and abilities with an eye toward guiding you toward the appropriate opportunities. This person could also help you with organizational processes, such as time management or programming the different tasks required to complete a project, or suggesting professional groups that could provide support materials and opportunities.

Group Practices

Today the demands on our field are so great that we must use every tool available to us, such as technological linkages and easier communication. Technology gives us extended opportunities for many design processes, but it can never replace personal relationships. We need the spirited contact and the stimulation of people who share our goals or who at least have complementary goals. We visit furniture markets and design shows for these reasons. But what do we have on a day-to-day basis?

Interior designers have always worked as independents, but this means we miss out on some opportunities. We've been deprived of social colleagues. That type of interaction is so important in nurturing the creative spirit, and it is missing when a designer sits in his or her own house, in his or her own studio, with no one else around. Designers who work in large firms have this, but the vast majority of interior designers do not.

We really need to associate with each other in some way, perhaps in a joint studio where designers could share materials and ideas. It's great sometimes to be at home and simply stick to a project until it is finished, but there are other times when being among people is more important. Working alone isolates us from ideas and intellectual stimulation needed to keep our skills up-to-date. A shared agent-career guide may create the sense of community we need.

We need to understand what our assets are in today's market and how they can be developed. This is one reason that an agent or professional career development resource could be helpful. Where will this human resource person come from? It could be an older designer who, as a leader, has had experience in creating opportunities for staff and other designers to develop their abilities.

An umbrella design agent-management firm could also provide some protection. As an example, interior designers could acquire good insurance programs, good retirement plans, and great types of backing in case they run into problems. We need some way to protect ourselves and offer the independent these type of services. Some benefits are available through professional associations. We can help each other with issues that may not be as formalized as insurance and retirement programs.

Working Globally

Professional magazines are always reminding us that there is a global market. Our resources are global. We can specify products from anywhere in the world just as easily as we do items from local craftspeople.

But let's be practical. You cannot leap into a global market without some preparation and a commitment for the long term. It's true that many designers have worked in other countries, and that some practices have become global in the last few years. And it is possible to duplicate a process you have done in the United States in another country, provided there is a team there that you can work with.

It is also possible to work with people outside the United States when they understand our culture or you understand theirs. But if you don't understand the language of the country you will be working in, you will be working with a handicap that is almost insurmountable. Corporations accept this; executives have been enrolling in language schools in increasing numbers.

The companies that today have offices in other countries planned ahead, the same intensive planning you went through when you started your business. Key people in the firm speak the languages and understand the cultures of the countries involved. Gensler & Associates Architects has 14 offices in the United States and abroad. Based in San Francisco, with a talent pool of multi-cultural designers to choose from, the company built relationships with many Pacific Rim countries. It took years.

Consider the very deep cultural and philosophical aspects of design work. Consider the communications problems that arise when both you and your client speak American English. Proxemics, the study of social and personal space and man's perception of it, is a key part of interior design. Edward Hall, the anthropologist who coined the term proxemics, said, "People from different cultures not only speak different languages, but inhabit different sensory worlds." It is hard for any participatory process to develop without the common ground of a shared language.

Even when you speak the language, cultural differences can stop you cold. There is a legendary story about American and British delegates arguing over whether to "table" a proposal. For the Americans, a "tabled" proposal was dead and done with. For the British, a tabled proposal was one that had been put on the table for discussion.

There's a great difference in "global" attitudes between the United States and Japan. When a U.S. company goes into a foreign country, they set up a factory that could run totally independent of the North American one. It may be run by native, non-North American officers. It's been designed to fit into that culture. With Japanese organizations, even if the factory is here in the United States, it is still controlled by Japan. The company culture is Japanese, and so is the hierarchy.

There was a time when the link between companies was political; now it's economical. A lot of designer resources have strong relationships with other countries because of the depth of their commitment to their investments in those countries. Japanese companies are still seen as foreign because they are directed by the homeland.

Firms that are realistically considering working in another country probably already have some tie-in. It may be with clients very well established both here and abroad. There may be resources you have worked with for years. Or perhaps you have always been fascinated with things of that culture and visit that country every time you get a chance.

In other words, there is a real commitment to working in that country. I'm not saying that it is impossible to work in other countries, but it is usually very costly and can be counter-productive, unless you make a long-term investment and become part of their culture.

There are several different levels of involvement in working abroad. Working abroad successfully takes a combination of people, knowledge of that particular country, and knowledge of outside resources that will assist in the process. You need three different kinds of people. First there are the explorers, the instigators, people who like to scout a new area and break the ice. Then there are the doers, who turn the instigators' dreams into reality. Finally, there are those who live in that country and maintain the relationship over a long period of time. This takes someone with deep financial pockets.

Establishing a base in another country often takes years. Building the understanding, the trust, and the working relationship needed for interior design doesn't happen overnight, and we shouldn't expect it to just because business analysts say it is possible to go global.

SPECIALTIES

Interior design is like any other service industry: find out what the client wants, and provide what he or she needs. Experience and judgment tell you what proportion of want to need makes up the project. Defining a direction for your firm involves the same sort of research and judgment. Firms positioned for business in the 1990s have carved out new specialties and revived old ones.

Professional design organizations have paid consultants to research the future for our industry, and the message is clear: narrow your focus, increase your depth of knowledge, and specialize! The ideal specialty combines elements of your own practice and personal interests. I'm not even going to try to list all the possible specialties, but here are some in which the demand seems to be growing.

Accessories Packaging

Developing a coordinated accessories program for retail furniture store vignettes has become a lucrative business. Designers arrange with the furniture manufacturer to design the wholesale showroom or gallery in exchange for space to exhibit the accessory packages. Typical packages fit style themes (safari, 18th century, English Country and Victoriana) and sell for under $5000. The accessories and props are a mix of mass produced and one-of-a-kind items. Retailers reorder through the firm that developed the package.

Acoustic Design

Sound is an integral part of every environment. Controlling sound and directing sound have become a science, and quiet has become a luxury. People often combine living and workspaces and must adapt sound control techniques developed for open landscape offices, including sound-breaking panels and sound maskers. Specialists in acoustic design consult on projects ranging from concert halls, conference rooms, open offices, and restaurants, to residential design. And there are specialists for each area.

When sound management is essential, this discipline may specify the shape of the room, lighting, and choice and placement of furnishings. In a teleconference room, it may include specifying the teleconferencing equipment. Teleconferencing on its own has been pinpointed as a hot specialty. One audio-video communications consulting firm says every project it works on is either installing teleconferencing equipment or making provisions for future installation.

Art Consulting and Dealing

Searching out existing art and contracting for art to be created for a specific environment is the function of the art consultant, who usually works for the client but may have been hired by the project interior designer or architect. A designer who specializes in art consulting usually does so to combine a love of fine art with the practical and artistic elements of interior design.

Interior designers with an interest in fine art understand what people enjoy and will buy. They understand the space, and they also know how to place art properly. These are major assets, because art sells best when it can be envisioned in or placed in an interior.

The trend today is for small galleries and brief shows. Sometimes the gallery is a tiny storefront. In New York City, "galleries" are sometimes the gallery owner's living room or spare bedroom and buyers view by appointment.

Aquarium Design

Small private aquariums are more than a design element or the client's discreet hobby. They are specified to reduce stress in offices, to set a mood in restaurants, or to call attention to displays in retail stores. Barney's, an upscale department store in New York City, displays jewelry and small accessories in special inserts in aquariums housed in wood-panelled storage units. The design specialist combines a fascination for fish with hands-on knowledge of carpentry and filtration systems.

Bathroom Design

Modern bathrooms may include spa-like environments with whirlpool baths, saunas, and hot tubs. These products come in a wide variety of materials, shapes, and sizes.

Public restrooms and bathrooms for commercial spaces demand state-of-the-art detailing. For areas meant to be used by many and varied people, the current trend is to specify plumbing that is triggered by light sensors.

Beauty and Barber Shop Design

Beauty and barber shops are often mixed-media salons, requiring space for services such as waxing, facials, manicures, and cosmetology, in addition to hair care. Some beauty salons are almost spa-like in their approach, offering massage, herbal wraps, mud-baths, child care, and light meals.

Regulations and requirements differ from state to state. Interior designers in the beauty field often work with or for suppliers, who may offer complete financing and turnkey projects.

Campus Design

Institutions of higher learning are not the only ones to need campuses. A corporate campus promotes efficiency and expresses the mission of the company through design tailored to meet the specific needs of that company. Campuses can include administration buildings, training centers, manufacturing or production facilities, and fitness centers. Some demand space that can be leased to support companies.

Designing a training center can be a specialty in itself. Adaptable lighting, accommodating audiovisual equipment, and attention to acoustics and sight lines are crucial elements.

The campus of a retirement community and nursing care facility includes facilities for assisted and unassisted living, community spaces such as cafeterias and card-rooms, and spaces for recreation. They may include long-term medical facilities.

Color Consultation

Color and its effects on people is a recognized science with well-documented results. Color is the most noticed of all the design elements. This specialty is used by all the design disciplines as well as marketing firms, corporations, governments, and medical practices—anywhere where encouraging specific reactions is desired.

Construction Management

One of the construction manager's primary goals is to improve the quality of the project, first by seeing to it that the specifications convey quality, and second by making sure that contractors and suppliers perform as promised. Working out the schedules for design and construction, the sequence of the work, cost control, value engineering, and system analysis are typical tasks. For this specialty to work, the roles of owner, architect, interior designers, engineers, suppliers, subcontractors, and construction manager are clearly spelled out on each project. In the role of contractor supervisors, interior designers may hire the architect, engineers, subcontractors, and consultants. They supervise, manage and review the components going into a project, and advise on decision-making. Interior designers are often hired to act as liaison between the contractor and client.

Country Club Design

These spaces combine aspects of residential and commercial design. The buildings must conform to area regulations and codes for fire, safety, labor, and industry. They must encourage proprietary feelings among the membership, but must also give the staff the tools to run programs with time and financial efficiency. Facilities may include indoor swimming pools, ball courts, gyms, locker rooms, restaurants, and areas for business meetings, celebrating, and socializing.

Design to Accommodate Pets

Pets are important to physical and mental health. Accommodating pets in a home involves a lot of common sense and may demand research on the particular pet. Some clients ask for playrooms for cats, dogs, ferrets, or iguanas.

Homes can accommodate pets and still be attractive. The system of narrow ramps and perches that keeps cats happy and active can be an artistic element along a wall. Aquariums can be built into wall systems in any style or period of furniture.

In the competitive world of breeding pedigreed pets, designing kennels for each species is a serious business. There are areas for grooming and training, food preparation and nutrition, as well as testing. Maintenance and health care are prime concerns.

Design for Children

Environment affects a child's behavior. Research indicates that what stimulates a child is different from what stimulates an adult. Spaces for children must be adaptable, because children change and grow so rapidly. These spaces are not just bedrooms and play areas, but include every place a child might use: doctor's offices, libraries, schools, and play areas in retail spaces.

Design of Community Spaces

This field encompasses lobbies and corridors of public and private buildings, luxury spaces for community and celebration, restaurant dining halls, training centers and convention spaces, guest rooms in hotels, the entries to malls, and more. Designers who specialize in communal spaces may do any or all of the types of spaces listed here.

Design for In-Home Medical Care

The trend is toward in-home care for patients with chronic, debilitating illnesses. There is also less risk of picking up new infections while their immunities are low, and the emotional comfort of being in one's own bed is important. This specialty means more than just installing a hospital bed. The residential space must be adapted to meet geriatric, orthopedic or other medical requirements of the patient. It should also be convenient for the caretakers.

Design for the Hearing- and Vision-Impaired

Not every person sees or hears well, and as we grow older both senses change. More than 60 percent of people in the work force have some hearing loss, and probably a larger percentage have some vision impairment. Some of the solutions are high tech; others are common sense. This specialty is getting more attention with the passage of the Americans with Disabilities Act (ADA). Some designers market this specialty as designing for the mature market.

Easy-Access, Barrier-Free Design for the Physically Limited

Easy-Access design is practical and desirable, but all too often it looks ugly. We know how to make ramps. How do we make them visually appealing so that people will use them? Design considerations for the physically limited also work for other disabilities. Wheelchair users ask that the doorsills not be used inside the home; this removes a tripping hazard for those with limited sight. Deaf workers ask that hallways in a new building be kept wide to accommodate signed conversations, and wider hallways have psychological benefits for everyone.

The ADA requires that new commercial and public buildings and renovations to these buildings be accessible to those in wheelchairs and those with other disabilities. It's likely that more money has gone into designing for the physically limited or orthopedically disabled than for any other group. This may be because most Americans have some experience with the physical limitations of a sprained or broken limb. Reviewing products and buildings for this group has become a specialty for some designers.

Energy-Efficient Design

An energy specialist advises on energy-efficient products and space planning for better use of energy. This can include adapting existing structures, or developing new ones, finding new uses for traditional products, and appropriate uses for new ones.

Energy efficiency, sun control, sunlight-resistant materials, and insulation are key points of designing for solar buildings. Coordinating solar and environmental concerns with human needs is a delicate balancing job, and the designer must moderate the client's real passion to save energy by making saving energy easy and practical.

The client's special interest in saving energy may mean that he or she is aware of more sources for low-energy products than most designers.

Environmental Audits

Many products and services fail to live up to their claims for easy operation and maintenance. This opens the door for a new special-ty: evaluating the operating efficiency of existing spaces. Possible criteria include quality of lighting, air, and acoustics; cost or man-hours per square foot for reconfiguration; average length of travel from key entrances or vertical transportation; accessibility of work stations to information; ease of operating specific facilities; and overall employee satisfaction. Efficiency can be measured by clients and credited to the interior design.

Ergonomic Design

Ergonomic design is the science that explores and documents the way people use things. While it began as an engineering science based on the physical needs of the human body and can include time-and-motion studies, it has become the buzzword for all com-fort factors in the workplace and at home. Factors considered are the measurements of the human body, human sensory capacities, comfort, body functions, safety, and emotional satisfaction.

In other words, a major portion of human factors is made up of information interior designers learned through experience. Now it is a science, and research papers provide statistical support for many of our decisions. A little research in human factors can enhance your appreciation for your own work, and you will be more able to communicate the value of design to your clients.

Ergonomics specialists are often called on to evaluate the way existing spaces function for the people who use them. Typically, one would evaluate the quality and variety of lighting in an office, the air quality, and space planning and traffic patterns. The specialist makes recommendations for change, giving the client options that are immediate, intermediate, and long term.

Facilities Management

Facility management services that could be provided by a design firm include fixed asset management, updated floor plans, inventories of furniture, fixtures, and equipment, base building evaluations, site and location studies, telecommunications and MIS coordination, real estate portfolio management and programming, planning, design, construction services, and project management.

Franchise Operations

Operating a franchise business permits interior designers to offer products and services beyond our individual capabilities. Franchises typically offer support, assistance regarding advertising, and name recognition. These days franchises are less restrictive; a person in one area may customize the products and services to a degree, but is still linked to a larger organization and has buying power, quick service, and the availability of special training.

Most franchises require a minimum of $100,000 or more to establish a business. Just as in other forms of business, fewer people will start a business with just a few dollars in their pockets. Anyone starting a business will have to be innovative to raise the capital.

The franchise investment offers a certain degree of insurance of success. A 1991 survey by Arthur Anderson indicates that 97 percent of franchisees survive over five years; not all surveys are this rosy in outlook. In general, working together and pooling information increase our chances of success. Franchises have this built into the system.

How can we bring a special product to the market and maintain our competitive advantage in our particular region? How can we acquire products at the best possible price, quickly? Some franchising programs offer 48-hour delivery on accessories and the prices are amazingly low. The quality seems to be good because there is definite control.

Investing in a franchise business is a way to take advantage of the skill and knowledge of professional buyers, who know how to buy in bulk and buy effectively. Look for cooperative buying franchises; they will often be connected by modern technology, providing more individual services and products at a very effective price.

Furniture Management

Furniture managers are similar in function to construction managers. They are responsible for negotiating all parts of the purchases for the installation, the trucking and warehousing, and any processes are related to the furnishings. When the construction manager is in the prebuilding phase, furniture managers are at work with the design team to develop specifications and suggest products. Typical services can include refining the budget, preparing documents and contracts, reviewing shop drawings and sample submissions, reviewing and monitoring the manufacturing process, and supervising the delivery installation.

The furniture manager does not take any commissions or mark-ups on the products, and is paid directly by the client. The fee earned by the furniture manager is considered by some clients to come out of the savings those services bring in. This is suitable on projects that usually run 50,000 square feet or more, and is extremely important to the larger projects. This became important during the 1980s and has continued because it is such an effective way to buy and deliver furnishings.

Greenhouses and Interior Landscaping

Plants add a natural quality to even the most static environment. They also clean and improve the indoor air quality. NASA has a list of plants and the specific chemicals they remove from the air. This field requires a knowledge of landscaping and botany to place plants where they are suitable. It may include contracting to provide maintenance and design changes for seasonal updates and plant health.

Interior plantscaping is an increasingly important component of a building's atmosphere. Design factors include temperature, light, and humidity control.

Health Club Design

Health clubs are more than places to exercise; they are meeting places for people with similar goals and interests. Athletic, aerobic, and recreational facilities of all sorts are proliferating, and they now include juice bars where club members can meet. Keeping the facilities safe, convenient, and appropriate to their specific sports is involved. The specialty has some aspects in common with country club design and with spa design.

Historic Preservation and Adaptive Reuse

This field demands technical and scientific knowledge. The research that determines the actual colors, materials, and wallcoverings attracts many designers. Adaptive reuse of older buildings—converting existing structures rather than razing them and building anew—can require integrating historic esthetics and modern functional requirements. Some areas offer substantial tax abatements for adaptive reuse.

While clients often ask for furnishings from a specific period, adhering too closely to what is historically correct may be uncomfortable and impractical. A knowledge of historic adaptations—

products recolored or rescaled for contemporary tastes and physical needs—can be useful.

Kitchen Design

Scientific and artistic detail go into the design and planning of components for residential and personal-use kitchens. The designer
must have a complete knowledge of currently available products as
well as the dietary requirements of the users.

Designing for commercial kitchens means you must know
about kitchen equipment and how to adapt it to the preferences of
individual restaurateurs. Kitchen specialists work as independents or for equipment suppliers. Kitchens for country clubs, educational facilities, and large commercial restaurants are typical
projects.

Library Design

Libraries are flexible, individual and specialized, catering to local
needs. A library in a county seat will be different from one on Wall
Street or one near a major hospital. Libraries need space planning
and marketing, with special attention to lighting and acoustics.
Many libraries have exhibit areas or function rooms. They are true
multimedia environments, lending books, videocassettes, art, and
music.

Electrical demands for libraries have increased greatly with the
advent of computers, which are used for card catalogs, periodical
indices, and subject-dedicated databases.

Light and Lighting

Lighting is a discipline unto itself. It is more than choosing the
right fixture or knowing the technical requirements and codes for
specific projects. Recent discoveries about light link the quality of
light to health. These studies indicate that the eye needs varying

light levels within a room, and that the best lighting imitates natural lighting.

Psychologists have documented a Seasonal Affective Disorder, the negative effects of which are moderated with special full-spectrum lighting. Dr. John Ott pioneered studies of the relationship of natural light and the healthy human. The information is easily available and the concepts easy to incorporate into design.

Lighting fixtures are a very important item in a room. Scale, structure, engineering, and a knowledge of the end use are critical components of good fixture design. In any space, your eye goes to the windows and to the lighting fixtures.

Medical Facilities Design

Hospitals, clinics, rehabilitative care centers, and nursing homes have needs and demands so specific and technologically complex that it is no longer possible to say you specialize in design for medicine. You must state a specific area, because only a specialist could keep up with the constant changes in standards, codes, and equipment. Areas for specialization include emergency rooms, intensive care units, lobbies, and administrative support.

Every medical specialty requires special equipment as well as appropriate space planning, traffic patterns, and storage management. The offices should be flexible enough to accommodate replanning in a few years, as equipment needs change quickly. A complete understanding of the medical procedures and equipment, legal aspects, codes, and aseptic demands is needed.

Multimedia Electrical Management

A knowledge of electronics, acoustics, and lighting is called for when designing rooms for the variety of electrical communications devices in the average home, business, or home-based business. Television, computer, fax machine, copier, videocassette recorder, and stereo equipment provide entertainment and worldwide communication for residential and commercial use.

Office Design

Home office design is the fastest growing segment of the office design industry, and some say it is the only segment that is growing. Whether the client is a one-man office or a corporation, the need is for flexible space with good wire control. This specialty requires a knowledge of high-tech equipment as well as an understanding of management and office production.

Park Design

Amusement, municipal, and other parks need safety, effective traffic patterns, management systems, and efficiency. Designers may be called on to develop unique signage, to design fixtures or service areas such as food service, restrooms, and souvenir shops. Some designers only work on theme parks.

Photographic Set Design

This specialty works with manufacturers and advertising agencies to create settings designed to sell products. The designers maintain an inventory of props and backgrounds, spend weeks creating and building a set, and tear it down immediately after photographing it. Successful photographic set design requires an understanding of what photographs well and what does not, as well as what can be faked.

Product Design, Evaluation, and Marketing

Interior design and industrial design must be blended for good product design. The interior designer knows where the furniture goes and how it is used; the industrial furniture designer knows construction techniques. The disciplines are merged in product design to develop products that are wanted, functional, and appropriate.

Interior designers with special knowledge of textiles design rugs, fabrics, and textile wallcoverings.

Purchasing

The designer as purchasing agent reviews and tests products, then negotiates and orders the furnishings.

Real Estate Development and Services

A knowledge of space, its uses, and its potential for change has given many interior designers an edge in real estate sales and development. Some designers assist developers by restructuring and designing buildings for turnkey or development projects.

With multiple-housing developments in every part of the country, this specialty presents major opportunities. Designing for real estate developers may be as simple as designing apartment layouts. There are may small specialties within this group, one for each type of room or space: lobbies, corridors, rooms for social gatherings, and athletic areas.

Interior designers work with landlords and developers to coordinate interior spaces for homes, apartments and commercial offices. The work includes color schemes and layouts, or may only make sure that the work of other designers coordinates with what exists in the building.

Many experienced designers have moved into upgrading luxury development homes. There is opportunity for creative design and it pays very well.

Some design firms furnish only model homes, renting or selling the components to contractors or developers for a specific period. The installations include all appointments, from table settings to towels for the bathroom—everything to create the impression that a real person lives there.

This is slightly different from a turnkey service, which may include everything from securing the property and designing and building the facility, to installing furnishings and finishing to the last detail. All the client needs to do is turn the key and open the door.

Rendering

Even though computer programs will insert items from catalog pages into a computer-generated rendering, hands-on rendering has not lost its appeal. It is a special art, requiring graphics, fine art, and design understanding. Even small design firms have projects for which a good rendering is needed. Fees can run into the thousands of dollars.

Residential Design

At one time considered the most prevalent design specialty, residential design also can be the most lucrative. It requires a knowledge of human behavior within living spaces, an understanding and ability to communicate with people, and the social respect of the client. Generally, people hire residential designers whose tastes and communications skills are similar to their own.

Retail and Specialty Selling

Selling is part of every design practice. Some designers have found it more lucrative to own, manage, or work for retail and specialty stores. Designers can be good sales people, especially now when consumers have expressed a desire for informed sales personnel. Interior designers may help develop a product mix for a specific store; this often means creating a design package to be sold by other people. It also can mean working with a group of artists to market their work.

Retail store design is a popular specialty that requires skill in image development, marketing, traffic patterns, and concern for financial return on space. Custom fixturing is often part of the design.

Communicating information is an essential part of selling today. Feeling the competition from catalogs and television shopping shows, store owners seek to regain their customers using the same tools that drew them away. Home-like product presentations, multimedia information, and graphic signage should be coordinated, and a designer who knows display design and acoustics can keep the information exchange from becoming just distracting noise.

A store or showroom must sell products; this is the primary job of the space. Whether it is beautiful is a question of taste, but whether it works and produces can be measured. Specialists in this field most often work in larger cities.

In mall design, each store must contribute to the total mall concept, and each mall tries to promote a different lifestyle or environment. Designers may work directly for the mall owners or with individual retailers, both on store design and on the common areas.

Retail Selling and the Design Studio

Because there are fewer places for clients to experience the way products work, design studios may have to incorporate some selling space or devise a shop-at-home service. If you can show the client a product sample in his or her space, very often you can sell it. Some shop-at-home services are franchised; others are run by designers with an intensive knowledge of a specific market. Some stock a van or truck with a coordinated line of pictures, accessories, pillows, and draperies.

Former stock broker Charlotte Moss took her last bonus and opened an American version of the English decorating shop, which sells products and design services under the same roof. The shop is designed to feel like a house, giving clients the opportunity to experience products as they would be used at home, and that stimulates ideas. "In a successful room, personality triumphs over decoration, and it is the little things that give a room personality."

Moss also applied her views to designing products for the furniture industry. Even the names of the furniture have personality. Century Furniture offers several signature pieces: a slipper chair, an Edwardian club chair, an ottoman, and a button-tucked society chair.

Sports Complex Design

While architects and engineers are most often involved with shaping the space, interior designers are consulted on public areas, service areas, and even the seating. This specialty is common with theater and store design: sight lines, traffic patterns, and graphic communication. Safety and security are also prime concerns.

Storage Design

Space is at a premium today, making planned storage an essential design element. Storage specialists catalog the clients' storables, then plan for growth. Custom storage can range from making tiny drawers to accommodate contact lenses to developing automated filing areas for offices of all sorts. Good storage means placing things in convenient locations near where they will be used, and putting lesser-used items in less accessible places. There are firms that do nothing other than plan and arrange closets.

Transportation Center Design

Airports and train and bus terminals have become almost total living environments, and they have a lot in common with theme parks. Interior designers are called on to create environments that entertain; accommodate specialty shops, ATMs, and small conference areas; offer traffic control and people movers; and house cocktail lounges and other food services. Waiting rooms typically offer coin-operated televisions and video games.

Wall Finishes

Marbling, fresco, and textured finishes—some of which have not been seen for centuries—are in demand. This specialty is no longer limited to historic restoration work; commercial and residential clients also request novel wall finishes. Concern for the environment and indoor air quality has created a demand for special paints and varnishes. The designer may need to find sources for ecologically correct finishes.

CHAPTER

14

MAP OR PLAN

DESIGN CAREER MAPPING

The challenge now is to redesign your business into a more vital entity, one that fulfills your need to create and meets the needs of the market today and tomorrow. You need the history of your business, your mission statement, and your answers to the hopes, dreams, and reality questionnaire. If you haven't done them, start now, because you cannot redesign your business without them.

Your first step is to list your accomplishments and abilities both as a firm and individually. Make lists of your successes and your values. What is your goal in being in business? This is your mission statement. Then dream a little. What would you really like to be doing in five years? Do your dreams fit with the realities of your business? What can you do to make your dreams achievable?

What do you need to do to complete your mission statement? You have defined what you do, your abilities, and what you want to do in the next three years. What steps should you plan to take?

You may need to change your staff.

You may need to purchase new tools or technology for your studio.

You may need to work on your client base. Probably you will need to work on all of these.

Goals, Dreams, and Reality

To find or create the perfect job as an interior designer, you need to have your goals and dreams in mind. Writing them down

211

sometimes helps refine them. Defining the problem is part of the solution.

1. What do you like to do?
2. What would you like the company to do for you?
3. If you could earn more money and do more of what you like, would you work for a company other than your own?
4. Is the design of your career pleasing? Is it going in the right direction?
5. Who are your preferred clients?
6. Do you like to develop and find your own clients or do you prefer someone else to do it for you?
7. What income would you like to earn?
8. What perks would you like to have?
9. What hours would you like to work?
10. What is your education and experience?
11. What type of projects have you done?

What do you have to do today to fulfill your mission statement? What do you have to change to meet your goals?

List the changes you need and the steps that will make them a reality, then rate them from one to ten as if we were designing a room instead of your future firm. When a client has a limited budget, we go through the project in terms of what needs to be done and how much it is going to cost; how we can invest money where it really counts. We have to look at our businesses in the same manner.

In the Reality Check sections, we targeted these issues, among others:

1. There are few places for consumers to see, feel, and test merchandise, yet products are available through many sources.
2. Clients have little time for extensive shopping; convenience is essential.

3. Clients are value-oriented.

4. Clients want fast service.

5. There are more home offices and smaller corporate spaces.

6. There is a large untapped mature market.

7. There is a huge body of information available to everyone through computers and modems.

At least one of these should call for change in your present studio. Whether you are in contract or residential design, between the availability and lack of availability of product types, you are finding a change in what your clients expect and the way you must conduct business. Because there are fewer places for consumers to experience furniture, our firm has devoted floor space to displaying upholstered furniture. I think in the future more and more design studios will adopt a sort of British decorating shop approach, selling products and services from the same space.

THE HISTORY OF THE FIRM

Writing a history of your firm will help you understand where you are today and provides a base to build on for the future. Create a history as if you were writing a biography of your firm. You don't have to do it all at once. Jot down some of your more memorable experiences and projects. What did you learn from them? Where did you go off-target? What projects led you in new directions?

Whether you choose to write your history on a computer or on a low-tech pad of paper, the history is something that will develop a project at a time. The best time to do a project history is when you finish the project. You tend to forget details over time.

Design Firm History

1. Start with the history of the founders: background and education, family's socio-economic background, the year the firm opened.

2. What experience did you have when you started your firm or joined this company? What year?

3. How did you get a financial base?

4. Why are you in interior design?

5. What is your work experience and areas of specialization?

6. What type of projects have you worked on?

7. List special accomplishments.

Design Career History

Record your progress with a yearly summary. If you have been in business a long time, you might want to do it in blocks of five years. This can be as simple or as complex as you want it. Your career design will need the following information.

1. What jobs did you accomplish? What jobs did you do? What did you accomplish on these jobs?

2. What did you learn from these jobs?

3. What was your method of working?

4. Did the clients become part of your design family?

5. Staff profile.

6. What resources were used and what do you think of them? Will you continue to use them?

7. Your consultants

8. Your financial profile

A pattern should emerge. You may find that early in your career you handled primarily small residential projects for people whose children were no longer living at home. Later on your practice might have concentrated on second homes or larger residential projects, or your firm took on a specialty. Some practices specializing in educational facilities began with kindergarten design but moved into the design of middle schools when the population changed.

Experience and Direction

What do you want to do in the near future? The following questions will help you define your direction.

1. What's your image? What makes your firm unique? Ask your clients.
2. What kinds of projects are you qualified to do?
3. What do you need to learn?
4. What are your methods of working?
5. What types of clients do you hope to make part of your design family?
6. Do you have the right skills on staff for what you want to do?
7. What consultants will your firm need?
8. What kinds of resources do you need to complete these projects successfully?

Career Development Worksheet

This is an annual assessment of your personal progress, what you learned as you worked on projects. At first, you may want to do a career development summary, then update it annually. Whether you are the firm's leader or an employee, just thinking about what you learned can be useful.

1. List the projects you have completed or were a part of.
2. List the benefits the firm's clients received from the firm's work and from your specific contributions.
3. Describe what you have learned through working at this firm for this time period.
4. Describe why you are more valuable today than you were a year ago.
5. List the new people who helped make it possible for you to work, and describe how they helped.

6. What new responsibilities or projects do you plan to take on in the next year?

7. What are your goals with this firm, and how do you plan to accomplish them?

Attach references from clients, vendors, and craftspeople as testimonials to the quality of your completed work. Include any relevant information about what you have accomplished in this time period.

This is the kind of information you need to plan a future for your firm, whether you do it for yourself or with a consultant. For the designers in my seminars, sometimes just the process of answering the questions suggested a new direction. Answering all the questionnaires should have given you an outline for a multiple action plan, a map for a possible future for your firm. It will need fine-tuning, and you will have to revise it as you go along.

It's not possible to do everything. With a Multiple Action Plan, you know where you have been and what you need to do to get where you want to be. You know what you are secure with and where you should spend your energies.

COACHING

Even though you may be entirely capable of devising your own Multiple Action Plan, consider using a consultant as a coach if you are considering changing or enhancing your business. The purpose of the coach-trainer is to empower the design professional to achieve higher levels of performance, greater job satisfaction, and greater profits.

A coach-trainer will help you see your firm's abilities more clearly, examine the behavioral influences of your staff and team members, and create a method for measuring progress. The first item on a trainer's agenda is a feasibility study, similar to the sort you do for each design project. The trainer will gather enough information to make a quality recommendation. From this, he or she will determine how much risk there is in following this course of action, and the ratio of risk to probable gain.

The trainer should help you develop a management system appropriate to your practices. Typically the management system will include built-in checks and balances, discuss the percentage of manual to automated work, and suggest technology and staffing. Other areas that should be covered are buying, marketing and selling (including business development and how to charge), team building, and money management. Continuing education and benchmarking are also included.

The relationship should continue with weekly or bi-weekly interaction to ensure that the program is working and to make necessary adjustments.

STRATEGY

Strategy is a group of integrated decisions that the leader-director of the firm or practice must make to position the business. These should be firm and clearly stated so that you, your staff, and your team will follow them without considering any other methods of working.

1. What is your present strategy?
2. What do you envision as the future of your business? How has it changed?
3. Considering the business today, is your present strategy a good one?
4. What are some other possible strategies? What are your options?
5. Which one of these options appeals most?
6. How can you create a usable strategy that includes your mission and vision statements? This is an essential part of developing a clear direction that is easy to follow.

The interior design business is customarily designed as an entrepreneurial structure. This means that it is headed by one person who has a group of people working with him or her. Even now that the style of business calls for increasingly equal roles in the team, there should be a leader or someone directing. This is probably the best system for most businesses. It permits the business to shift and change with the environment, without cumbersome bureaucratic procedures or the chaos of no leadership.

The business strategy must include all of these components:

1. Product. Define the product that you are selling.

2. Market. What clients will want and need what you have to sell?

3. Price structure. How are you going to charge? Retail? Will you charge for hourly rates or set fees?

4. Service. What services do you need to provide to bring a product to the given market?

5. Sources. What sources do you have access to? Where will you get the product from and how good are your links to those sources? How reliable are they?

6. Distribution. What will the process of distribution be? How are you going to get merchandise to the client?

7. Team. Who is on the team and how can you count on them? What part do they play in the business?

8. Facility. What type of facility do you need to display and store your product? Do you need a showroom, a studio, or something else? Does your type of practice demand high visibility and easy access or could you work out of the second floor of a garage?

9. Financial. What kind of capital do you need? What will your cash flow be? Where does the money come from, where does it go, and what is left in the end?

10. System of operation. If you are going to make this work properly, what type of system do you need, what are your checks and balances?

11. Technology. How does technology affect the market? Is it changing your market? What kind of technology do you need in your studio? Figure out where technology fits, both internally and externally, in your business.

12. Learning resources. If you are going to acquire knowledge and be part of the research process and learn from other companies, what is your resource plan?

13. Legal issues. What are the legal issues that you should expect to deal with? There are regulations that you must abide by as well as many other issues.

14. Leadership. Who is the leader? Someone has to lead and direct. Who is the person you will choose and where will they fit within the structure you have chosen?

ACTION ITEMS

Time Management

Time management has less to do with controlling time than with controlling events, according to Hyrum W. Smith, Chairman and CEO of the Franklin Quest Co., a time management firm. Smith says the secret of controlling events is to relate them to your personal values.

Where do you want to spend time and what do you want to do? Smith, like Stephen R. Covey, author of *The Seven Habits of Highly Effective People*, suggests that you list your most important values, then organize your schedule around these values. Covey suggests you further break things down into urgent and important.

There will always be interruptions and demands. If the demand helps any of your governing values, change your schedule. The key to peace of mind is letting your values direct your schedule. In other words, schedule your priorities.

Covey lists three generations of time management. The first advises you to go with the flow but keep track of the things you do, checking off items on a list as you accomplish them. The second is planning and preparation: making appointments, identifying deadlines, and noting where meetings are held. The third is planning, prioritizing, and controlling. After spending time clarifying your values, you are asked to set long-, medium- and short-term goals to obtain these values.

Do you really believe that time management puts you in control? We live in the real world with real people, who cannot be controlled. Does it make you more efficient? Of course. You get more done, faster. Just ask yourself if it is in the right direction. And plugging in your values isn't the whole answer, because values don't necessarily have anything to do with the quality of life.

Covey: "Traditional time management focuses on getting what you want and not letting anything get in the way." Other people are seen either as resources or obstacles, and relationships are transactional as opposed to transformational. He suggests that a fourth generation of time management is called for: knowing what is important, instead of simply responding to what is urgent.

This fourth generation of time management is most closely attuned to today's business management theories. Says Covey, "You manage things, but you must lead people."

Benchmarking

Benchmarking and other management programs provide a system and structure that can help you create your own best operating procedures. It is possible to create a good system of management through inspiration, trial and error, experience, and luck. You can have a firm that works well without having studied any specific management program. However, when you design a room, you often use creative adaptation of ideas you have collected from perhaps a hundred different places. These "borrowed" ideas are a jumping off point for creative thought. That is the idea behind benchmarking: that it takes less time to build on the ideas of others than to start fresh from the ground up. Why should you duplicate effort when you can get farther faster by learning from others and going beyond their efforts?

Benchmarking is an ongoing activity; the goal is to identify the best operating practices. You don't set an arbitrary standard for quality in your firm; you investigate the competition and your own firm and study the internal and external practices that lead to better performance. In benchmarking, you build on your own past successes and learn from the success of others. In any benchmarking or management plan, make sure the project has a clear focus.

In *Benchmarking for Best Practices*, Christopher Bogan and Michael English identify three types of benchmarking. Process benchmarking focuses on specific work processes and operating systems. Performance benchmarking rates competitive position by targeting price, technical quality, product or service features, and other performance characteristics. Strategic benchmarking tries to identify winning strategies that enable high performing companies in any industry to succeed.

The program lets you know where your firm stands in relation to the best in the industry. It creates a fast-learning culture dedicated to continuous improvement, supports strategic planning, and helps accomplish organizational restructuring. Benchmarking works. It has a proven track record in firms such as Motorola, General Electric, Ford, and Xerox. It provides external reference points so that your strategic planning is not the equivalent of flying blind.

Benchmarking is the continuous process of measuring products, services and practices against the toughest competitors or those companies recognized as industry leaders.

DAVID KEARNS, former CEO of Xerox

Study the Competition

Study your competition. It may point you toward a new segment of the market, or steer you away from it.

If your competition is so heavily invested in a specialty that they can perform it better and for a lesser cost than you could, it might be wise to stay out of that area of business unless you are willing to make an equal or more extensive investment than they have.

Who and what kind of consultants do they add to their teams? Looking at who your competition chooses as partners can be revealing. You may want to use some of the same consultants, because they have a track record in working with designers. Then again, the relationship between the outside professionals and the competition may be so strong that you need to look elsewhere for potential team members.

Who in your firm should study the competition? It makes sense to let your newest employee shop another store or another office, but it takes someone with a knowledge of your business to really be able to understand what the competition is doing. Ideally this person will also know people within the competing firm from previous work associations, and can talk with them. In the end, it may take everyone on your firm to gather information that you or the team leader will analyze.

Some information about your competition can be found in database information accessible by many computers, in newspapers and magazines, and other public records. Newspapers and magazines often list projects awarded to firms, the square footage, and the nature of the project. Installation stories can tell you how a design firm handled a specific problem. A company's stated philosophy of business is generally part of any profile in the business pages of the newspaper. Sometimes the society pages provide clues to which designers are allied with which potential clients.

You also learn about your competition by attending meetings of professional organizations and by talking with other competitors, often about things not directly related to interior design. Clients will often tell you at length how they liked a project, what worked and what didn't work, and what it is like to work with your competition.

Studying the competition is simply being aware of movement in your market.

POSTSCRIPT

What's happening in the design industry today is exciting, chaotic, terrifying, and exhilarating. The industry is full of opportunities.

No one person has all the answers. I hope that this book will encourage every designer and all those in related fields to start examining the opportunities. It's time to recognize that design is synonymous with leadership. We are *ready* for a change. We have a field with a strong core of knowledge, a great spirit, and a soul. Interior design has the power to change lives. Use it responsibly.

NOTES

CHAPTER 2

Page 12. Marsha Sinetar, *Do What You Love, the Money Will Follow: Discovering Your Right Livelihood*, New York: Paulist Press, 1986.

CHAPTER 3

Page 19. Michael Hammer and James Champy, *Reengineering the Corporation: A Manifesto for Business Revolution*, New York: Harper Business, 1993, p. 32.

———. "The office furniture firm of Haworth saved . . . from employees in 1993." "Haworth Employees Save Company $" *The Monday Morning Quarterback*, June 26, 1994, p. 2.

———. "Open-space meetings are a version of management by team." Claudia H. Deutsch, "Round Table Meetings With No Agendas, No Tables," *The New York Times*, June 5, 1994, p. 5.

Page 20. "American workers are better than you think." "The American Worker Is Better Than You Think," *Central Penn Business Journal*, May 6, 1994, p. 5.

Page 21. "Jay Chiat, president of the . . . traditional offices to kindergarten." *The Monday Morning Quarterback*, July 1993, p. 2.

Page 22. "In Manhattan, the 275-member accounting firm of Ernst & Young . . . officeless office." Phil Patton, "The Virtual Office Becomes Reality," *The New York Times*, October 28, 1993, p. C1:5.

———. "You're sending some very clear signals to people that they're simply an extension of some sort of machine." Mary Kane "It's a Brave New Corporate Space," *Harrisburg Patriot*, June 13, 1994, p. B2.

Page 23. "A Chicago apartment complex, ParkShore . . . office center in an upscale apartment building." Charles Pappas, "New Services for Renters," *Home Office Computing*, June 1994, p. 16.

CHAPTER 4

Page 28. "Tom Peters praised the design industry in his book *In Search of Excellence* ten years ago, citing Herman Miller as a positive example." *The Monday Morning Quarterback*, September 27, 1993, p. 2.

——. "In the apparel industry, a certain percentage of each line is designed for runway success only; its real purpose is to generate publicity that may cause buyers to rethink the line." Mark McIntyre, "Selling Innovative Design," *Interior Design*, January 1991, p. 42.

——. Michael K. Dugan. "Good design is salable." Harvey Probber, "Executive Involvement in the Design Process," *Interior Design*, May 1990, pp. 62–64.

Page 29. Roger Yee, "It's Cheap — and It's No Good!" *Contract Design*, May 1994, p. 8.

Page 30. ". . . Epperson says 1994 will be the year of the electronic retailing of furniture." Patricia Bowling, "Alternative Channels of Distribution? Jerry Epperson Debunks the Myths," *Home Furnishings Executive*, April 1994, p. 49.

——. "Industry observer Jerry Epperson believes distribution is perhaps the greatest factor in the success of any furniture manufacturer." Bowling, p. 43.

Page 31. "The disparity in pricing gives consumers the impression that price is the main issue in whether to buy." Patricia N. Bowling, "Discount Pricing, A Blow to Credibility?" *Home Furnishings Executive*, April 1994, pp. 56–60.

Page 32. "Today, outfitting a room is not a user-friendly experience." Cheryl and Jeffrey Katz, "The Ideal Home Store," *Accessories Merchandising*, June 1994, p. 24.

——. "In response to consumer demand, some furniture retailers have begun to sell accessories as well." Kimberly Wray, "Showing Its Stripes: Waverly Place Gives Furniture Stores a Pattern for Success," *High Points*, April 11, 1994, pp. 56–58.

Page 35. "Christopher Kennedy . . . says the answer lies in viewing the consumer, rather than architects and designers, as the ultimate client in the distribution channel." Kristen Richards, "Design Centers: Public or Private?" *Interiors*, April 1994, pp. 30–36+.

——. "The president of Steelcase challenged his people to come up with different ways to help the clients. Haworth has a room of test products: among them the office/locker, for people who share office space, and the office in a cubicle, for rentals at transit centers." *The Monday Morning Quarterback*, April 11, 1994, pp. 1, 2.

CHAPTER 5

Page 37. Gerald Celente, *Trend Tracking*, New York: John Wiley, 1990, p. 13.

Page 38. Michael Maren, "Predict the Future and Profit," *Home Office Computing*, January 1994, p. 54–58.

Page 39. "'You can't make money as an entrepreneur 20 years ahead,' says Dychtwald." Quoted in Maren, p. 58.

Pages 45–46. "For Knoll's Parachute chair, a hundred people of different sizes and occupations. . . ." "Form + Function," *Wall Street Journal*, May 2, 1994, p. B1.

Page 48. "CAD is moving into consumer applications. . . ." "Virtual Home," *The New York Times*, Home Design, April 10, 1994, p. 11.

Page 49. "With a wheelchair simulator . . . a planned 14-room hospital installation." David Cinelli, "Using Virtual Reality for Interior Design," *Interiors & Sources*, September 1993, pp. 88–91.

CHAPTER 6

Page 55. "Statisticians claim we work an average of a hundred thousand hours in a traditional lifetime, and that this takes 47 years." Juliet Schor, *The Overworked American: The Unexpected Decline of Leisure*, New York: Basic Books, 1991.

———. "Between 1977 and 1989, incomes changed." "The Design Business Outlook for 1994," *Contract Design*, January 1994, pp. 66–72.

Page 56. "Income per capita has increased, but income per person has dropped." Ben Stein, "Why We're Poorer and Richer," *New York*, April 11, 1994, p. 14.

Page 57. "Kitchens are now the family room. . . ." *Window Fashions*, August 1993, pp. 30–32.

Pages 62–63. Shauna Corry and Joann Asher Thompson, *The Journal of Interior Design*, Volume 19, No.2, 1993, p. 31.

CHAPTER 7

Page 68. "The value of a well-designed environment is verifiable. . . ." "Vision 2010," *Interiors & Sources*, June 1994, p. 20.

Page 70. "One thing we can offer is a livability assessment of the spaces, views, storage, and multiple functions a home is expected to harbor." Roger Yee, "No Respect," *Contract Design*, August 1993, p. 8.

———. "Gensler & Associates Architects . . . is growing. The firm heads *Interior Design* magazine's list of biggest firms." Glenn Rifkin, "Efficiency, Not Ego, Gives Edge to Design Firm," *The New York Times*, April 10, 1994, p. F7.

Page 71. "Tom Peters also says that design should take an equal and early seat at the head table, on board at the creation of the dream and an equal partner throughout." Tom Peters, "It's Design, Stupid, That Sets Objects Apart," *Central Penn Business Journal*, May 30, 1994.

Page 73. Roger Yee, "Are You an Artist or a Designer?" *Contract Design*, June 1993, p. 8.

Page 74. "Interior designers have been described as operating at a pre-empirical intuitive level, but we don't have to design by hunch and guesswork today." Robert Sommer, *Personal Space: the Behavioral Basis of Design*, Englewood Cliffs: Prentice-Hall Spectrum. 1969, p. 6.

——. "Many of the insights . . . come from the sociology and psychology fields." John Pile, *Interior Design*, New York: Abrams, 1988, p. 374.

CHAPTER 8

Page 82. Sherrill Whiton, *The Elements of Interior Decoration*, New York: Lippincott, 1944, p. 5.

——. Edward T. Hall, *The Hidden Dimension*, New York: Doubleday-Anchor, 1966, p. 181.

——. Pile, p. 373.

Page 90. "'Designers' knowledge of aesthetics. . . . No one with a physical difference wants to be stigmatized by that difference.'" Quoted in Diane Wintroub Cameron, "Simply Good Design," *Interiors & Sources*, January 1994, pp. 28–32.

CHAPTER 9

Page 113. Joe Batten, "A Total Quality Culture," *Management Review*, May 1994, p. 61.

Page 123. "Power: a Harvard Expert Reveals How to Win." Howard H. Stevenson and Michael Warshaw, *Success*, June 1994, p. 36.

CHAPTER 10

Page 134. ". . . the big three auto makers told universities to stop turning out traditional engineers." Paul A. Eisenstein, "Big Three Automakers Aiming to Change Education," *Investor's Business Daily*, March 4, 1994, p. 4.

Page 136. "AMP . . . has a training program that communicates what the internal experts know." Joseph Giusti, "Training Keeps AMP Connected to Customers," *Training & Development Journal*, October 1990, pp. 73–79.

Page 139. Addresses for professional organizations:
American Society of Interior Designers (ASID)
608 Massachusetts Ave.
Washington, DC 20002

International Interior Design Association (IIDA)
341 Merchandise Mart
Chicago, Il 60654

Page 141. "Design educator Nick Politis says that probably only half of what designers need to know is learned in the classroom. . . ." Laura Mayer, "One on One with Nick Politis," *Contract*, December 1989, pp. 32–33.

CHAPTER 11

Page 162. Howard Rheingold, *The Virtual Community*, Reading, MA: Addison-Wesley, 1993, p. 59.

CHAPTER 12

Page 179. ". . . the next time a job candidate dozes off during the interview, wake him up and hire him." Tom Peters, "Peters on Excellence," *Central Penn Business Journal*, April 18, 1994, p. 45.

CHAPTER 13

Page 192. "Gensler & Associates Architects has 14 offices. . . ." Rifkin, p. F7.

———. Edward T. Hall, *The Hidden Dimension*, p. 6.

CHAPTER 14

Page 219. Hyrum W. Smith, "Simple Secrets of Time Management," *Boardroom Reports*, April 1, 1994, p. 13.

———. Stephen Covey, *Success* magazine, special book bonus excerpt, April 1994.

BOOK LIST

Abercrombie, Stanley. *A Philosophy of Interior Design*. New York: Harper and Row, 1990.

Aburdene, Patricia and John Naisbitt. *Megatrends for Women*. New York: Villard Books 1992.

Albrecht, Karl. *The Northbound Train*. New York: AMACON, 1994.

Armstrong, David M. *Managing by Storying Around: A New Method of Leadership*. New York: Currency-Doubleday, 1992.

Annison, Michael H. *Managing the Whirlwind*. Englewood, CO: Medical Group Management Association, 1993.

Attali, Jaques. *Millenium—Winners and Losers in the Coming World Order*. New York: Times Books, 1991.

Belasco, James A. *Teaching the Elephant to Dance: Empowering Change in Your Organization*. New York: Crown, 1990.

Bennis, Warren G. *On Becoming a Leader*. New York: Addison-Wesley, 1989.

———. *On Becoming a Leader*. Chicago, IL: Nightingale-Conant Corporation, 1991. (tape)

———. *An Invented Life: Reflections on Leadership and Change*. Reading, MA: Addison-Wesley, 1993.

Block, Peter. *Stewardship: The Triumph of Service over Self-Interest or Choosing Service Over Self-Interest*. San Francisco, CA: Berrett-Koehler, 1993.

Bogan, Christopher and Michael English. *Benchmarking For Best Practices*. New York: McGraw Hill, 1994.

Byham, William C., Ph.D., and Jeff Cox. *Heroz: Empower Yourself, Your Coworkers, Your Company*. New York: Harmony Books, 1994.

Carlson, Richard, and Bruce Goldman. *Fast Forward: Where Technology, Demographics, and History Will Take America and the World in the Next Thirty Years*. New York: HarperBusiness, 1994.

Carnegie, Dale, and Associates, Inc. *The Leader in You*. New York: Simon and Schuster, 1994.

Celente, Gerald, with Tom Milton. *Trend Tracking: The System To Profit From Today's Trends.* New York: Warner Books Inc., 1990.

Covey, Stephen R. *The Seven Habits of Highly Effective People: Restoring the Character Ethic.* New York: Simon and Schuster, 1983.

————. *Principle-Centered Leadership.* New York: Summit Books, 1991.

Davis, Stanley M. *Future Perfect.* New York: Addison-Wesley, 1987.

DePree, Hugh D. *Business as Unusual.* Zeeland, MI: Herman Miller, Inc., 1986.

DePree, Max. *Leadership Is an Art.* New York: Doubleday, 1989.

Dent, Harry S. Jr. *The Great Boom Ahead.*

Dilenschneider, Robert L. *On Power.* New York: HarperBusiness, 1994.

Drucker, Peter F. *Managing a Non-Profit Organization.* New York: HarperCollins, 1990.

————. *Post Capitalist Society.* New York: HarperBusiness, 1993.

Edelston, Martin and Marion Buhagiar. *I-Power—The Secrets of Great Business in Bad Times.* Fort Lee, NJ: Barricade Books, 1992.

Flamholtz, Eric G. *Growing Pains.* San Francisco, CA: Jossey-Bass, 1990.

Goldratt, Eliyahu M., and Jeff Cox. *The Goal.* St. Paul, MN: Penguin-High Bridge Audio, 1992.

Gross, Ronald. *The Independent Scholar's Handbook.* Berkeley, CA: Ten Speed Press, 1993.

Hall, Edward T. *The Hidden Dimension.* New York: Doubleday-Anchor, 1966.

Handy, Charles. *The Age of Paradox.* Boston, MA: Harvard Business School Press, 1994.

Hammer, Michael, and James Champy. *Reengineering the Corporation: A Manifesto for Business Revolution.* New York: Harper Business, 1993.

Hanon, Mack. *Tomorrow's Competition: The Next Generation of Growth Strategies.* New York: AMACOM, 1991.

Hickman, Craig R. *Mind of a Manager, Soul of a Leader.* New York: John Wiley, 1990.

————. *The Oz Principle: Getting Results Through Individual and Organizational Accountability.* Englewood Cliffs, Prentice-Hall 1994.

Johnson, Spencer. *Yes or No: The Guide to Better Decisions.* New York: HarperCollins, 1992.

Kaztenbach, Jon R., and Douglas K. Smith. *The Wisdom of Team: Creating the High Performance Organization.* New York: Harper Business School Press, 1994.

Kouzes, James M., and Barry Z. Posner. *The Leadership Challenge: How To Get Extraordinary Things Done In Organizations.* San Francisco, CA: Jossey-Bass, 1987.

Krugman, Paul. *Peddling Prosperity: Economic Sense and Nonsense in the Age of Diminished Expectations.* New York: W.W. Norton, 1994.

Liebig, James E. *Merchants of Vision: People Bringing New Purpose and Value to Business*. San Fransisco, CA: Berret-Koehler, 1994.

Lipnack, Jessica, and Jeffrey Stamps. *The Team Net Factor: Bringing the Power of Boundry Crossing into the Heart of Your Business*. Essex Junction, VT: Oliver Wright, 1993.

Lofland, Donald J. *Powerlearning: Memory and Learning Techniques and Personal Power*. Stanford, CT: Longmeadow Press, 1992.

McCarthy, Michael J. *Mastering the Information Age: A Course in Working Smarter, Thinking Better and Learning Faster*. Los Angeles, CA: Jeremy P. Tarcher, 1991.

Naisbitt, John. *Global Paradox: The Bigger the World Economy, the More Powerful its Smallest Players*. New York: William Morrow, 1994.

Naisbitt, John, and Patricia Aburdene. *Megatrends 2000: Ten New Directions for the 1990's*. New York: William Morrow, 1994.

John N. Ott. *Light, Radiation and You*. Greenwich: Devin Adair Publishers, 1982.

Peppers, Don, and Martha Rogers. *The One-to-One Future: Building Relationships, One Customer at a Time*. New York: Currency Doubleday, 1993.

Peters, Thomas J. *Thriving on Chaos: A Handbook for a Managment Revolution*. New York: Alfred A. Knopf, 1987.

———. *Liberation Management: Necessary Disorganization for the Nanosecond Nineties*. New York: Alfred A. Knopf, 1992.

———. *The Seminar: Crazy Times Call For Crazy Organizations*. New York: Vintage Books, 1994.

Phillips, Donald T. *Lincoln in Leadership: Executive Strategies for Tough Times*. New York: Warner Books, 1992.

Pile, John. *Interior Design*. New York: Abrams, 1988.

Ray, Michael, and Alan Renzler. *The New Paradigm in Business: Emerging Stategies for Leadership and Organizational Change*. New York: Jeremy P. Tarcher/Perigree, 1993.

Robertson, Pamela, ed. *Charles Rennie Mackintosh: The Architectural Papers*. Cambridge: MIT Press, 1990.

Roddick, Anita. *Body and Soul: Profits and Principles*. New York: Crown Publishers Inc., 1991.

Seashore, Charles N., Edith Whitfield Seashore, and Gerald M. Weinberg. *What Did You Say? The Art of Giving and Receiving Feedback*. North Attleborough, MA: Douglas Charles Press, 1992.

Senge, Peter M. *The Fifth Discipline: The Art and Practice of the Learning Organization*. New York: Currency Doubleday, 1990.

Senge, Peter M., Charlotte Roberts, Richard B. Richards, J. Bryan and Art Kleiner. *The Fifth Discipline Fieldbook: Strategies for Building a Learning Organization*. New York: Currency Doubleday, 1994.

Spendolini, Michael J. *The Benchmarking Book.* New York: AMACOM, 1992.

Stanley, Thomas J. *Marketing to the Affluent.* Homewood, IL: Dow Jones-Irwin, 1988.

————. *Selling to the Affluent.* Homewood, IL: Business One Irwin, 1991.

Toffler, Alvin. *Powershift: Knowledge, Wealth and Violence at the Edge of the 21st Century.* New York: Bantam Books, 1990.

Tomasko, Robert M. *Rethinking the Corporation: The Architecture of Change.* New York: AMACOM, 1993.

Waterman, Robert H., Jr. *What America Does Right: Learning from Companies that Put People First.* New York: W.W. Norton, 1994.

Weiner, Edith, and Arnold Brown. *Office Biology: Why Tuesday is Your Most Productive Day and Other Relevant Facts for Survival in the Workplace.* New York: MasterMedia Limited, 1993.

Wertzen, H. Skip. *Hypergrowth.* New York: John Wiley & Sons, 1991.

Weston, J. Fred, and Eugene F. Brigham. *Essentials of Managerial Finance.* 7th ed. Hinsdale, IL: Dryden Press, 1985.

Whiton, Sherill. *Elements of Interior Decoration.* New York: Lippincott, 1944.

INDEX